SINGLE-SUBJECT EXPERIMENTAL RESEARCH:

APPLICATIONS FOR LITERACY

Susan B. Neuman and
Temple University

Sandra McCormick
The Ohio State University

Editors

International Reading Association
800 Barksdale Road, PO Box 8139
Newark, Delaware 19714-8139, USA

The International Reading Association attempts, through its publications, to provide a forum for a wide spectrum of opinions on reading. This policy permits divergent viewpoints without assuming the endorsement of the Association.

Director of Publications   Joan M. Irwin
Managing Editor   Anne Fullerton
Associate Editor   Christian A. Kempers
Assistant Editor   Amy L. Trefsger Miles
Editorial Assistant   Janet Parrack
Production Department Manager   Iona Sauscermen
Graphic Design Coordinator   Boni Nash
Design Consultant   Larry Husfelt
Desktop Publishing Supervisor   Wendy Mazur
Desktop Publishing   Anette Schütz-Ruff
                                        Cheryl Strum
Proofing   David Roberts

Library of Congress Cataloging in Publication Data
    Single-subject experimental research: Applications for Literacy/Susan B. Neuman, Sandra McCormick
        p.   cm.
    Includes bibliographical references and indexes.
    1. Education—Research—Methodology.   2. Single subject research.
3. Literacy—Research—Methodology.   I. Neuman, Susan B.
II. McCormick, Sandra.
LB1028.S512   1995   94-45949
370'.78—dc20   CIP
ISBN 0-87207-128-6

FOR DAVID, SARA, AND TOM

Contents

Foreword

As theory evolves and guides educational research and practice, so do the methods that seem most appropriate for investigation. In the field of literacy education, we are seeing some convergence in theory around a set of socially oriented views frequently characterized as social-constructivist, sociolinguistic, sociocultural/historical. This convergence in thinking has led to a reexamination of the potential uses for research methods that traditionally have been tied to a particular conceptual model or perspective. Consistent with this trend, this volume examines single-subject research not so much from the perspective of a particular conceptual framework or belief system, but more in the spirit of developing a repertoire of methods to address a variety of research questions.

The questions raised within the behaviorist tradition, which gave rise to single-subject research, often focused on identifying consistent effects of various interventions across students. In contrast, current socially oriented conceptualizations are concerned more with questions regarding the variability that occurs in literacy learning and literate behavior both within and among students. So, rather than asking which method is most effective, we are now asking which method is most effective for a particular student within a specified context, or how different students perform under different instructional conditions.

Single-subject research methods enable one to describe the variability predicted by current theory more precisely than is often possible with either group experiments or thick descriptions. This is important both for better informed practice and to help push our thinking and our theories. We must also remember, however, that as our questions change, so does our understanding of the problems associated with using research methods for purposes other than those for which they have been traditionally employed.

This volume fills an important need by examining the application of single-subject research to literacy education within contemporary theoretical and methodological contexts. The material is sufficiently detailed to help someone new to this area get started, but not so technical as to discourage newcomers from experimenting with this method. Finally, the presentation of information reflects the versatility of the method itself, which should go a long way toward promoting interest in a method of research that has a lot to offer the field of literacy education.

Karen K. Wixson

Preface

Although studies of the individual have always had a place in educational and psychological research, investigations involving single subjects have become increasingly popular in recent years. Traditionally, single-subject experimental research has been useful in clinical applications where the focus is on the therapeutic value of an intervention for the client. However, recent applications of single-subject research in areas such as literacy, language education, and cognitive psychology suggest that these designs provide a powerful way of examining interventions, particularly when reporting average differences for groups may have little meaning. Moreover, researchers are increasingly turning to an analysis of single subjects in conjunction with other research techniques as a way of explicating findings, providing a more integrated and detailed analysis of the impact of interventions.

Why study the individual subject? For one, this approach allows researchers to examine the effects of an experimental treatment or treatments when it is difficult to obtain groups of subjects, or when comparability among and between groups is difficult to establish. It can bypass an error often found in group-comparison studies—intersubject variability—because each individual serves as his or her own control. In addition, single-subject designs provide researchers with information on what may be important differences among individuals. For example, although a particular technique might work best for many students, for others an alternative technique may be superior. Further, with replication, the researcher can determine whether the intervention is effective for other individuals and in other settings, helping him or her to build important theoretical links in establishing generalizability.

Single-subject experimental design, however, should not be confused with case-study methods. Although both case studies and single-subject experiments study the individual, in a single-subject experiment the investigator deliberately manipulates one or more independent variables. Single-subject experiments are designed to generate functional and causal statements, whereas case studies are designed to provide insight by describing phenomena.

This book is written for language and literacy researchers—novices as well as those experienced in more traditional experimental designs—as an introduction to single-subject experimental designs. The authors describe the most common procedures, uses, and multiple applications (what unique questions may be answered, and how these questions may be researched and analyzed), weaving examples of literacy studies throughout to emphasize these applications. In each chapter, design strengths and limitations are discussed, as well as important considerations of validity, reliability, and generalizability as applied to them.

The book begins with a chapter by McCormick, describing the basic principles and underlying parameters of single-subject experimental research. Subsequent chapters by Yaden, Kucera and Axelrod, and Neuman focus on the three most common designs, including reversal (Chapter 2), multiple-baseline (Chapter 3), and alternating-treatments (Chapter 4) designs. Each of these chapters describes several variations within designs and focuses on how they might be used to explore questions in literacy. Chapter 5 tackles the important issue of applying statistical techniques in single-subject designs. Although single-subject researchers have traditionally relied on the visual analysis of data, Kamil describes under what conditions statistical comparisons may be particularly appropriate and useful.

Chapters 6 and 7 move beyond a description of the methodology to its application in combination with other methodologies and in classroom settings. Bisesi and Raphael (Chapter 6) examine the traditions of quantitative research (with a special emphasis on single-subject designs) and qualitative research, and suggest key ways in which these methods may be combined. Braithwaite (Chapter 7) discusses how single-subject designs may be used as a tool for the teacher-researcher to enhance understanding of literacy processes for individual students in the classroom. Palincsar and Parecki (Chapter 8) conclude with an examination of strategies to address important issues of validity and reliability in relation to single-subject experimental research.

This book is designed as a practical guide. Our goal is to provide researchers with an additional methodological tool to examine critical questions in literacy. In this respect, we hope to generate interest in new ways to inquire, expanding and stimulating further explorations in language and literacy development.

SBN

SM

CHAPTER 1

What Is Single-Subject Experimental Research?

Sandra McCormick

Anyone unacquainted with single-subject experimental research probably has at least two fundamental questions about it:

1. *Do investigations guided by this research model include only a lone subject?*
Answer: Sometimes, but often not.

2. *Can traditional experimental methodologies be applied if there is only one subject in a study (or if there are only a very few subjects)?*
Answer: Somewhat, but not exactly.

This chapter will explain these answers further and introduce you to important parameters for conducting single-subject literacy studies.

The Purposes of Single-Subject Experimental Research

The aim of single-subject experimental research is to clearly establish the effects of an intervention (that is, an independent variable) on a single individual. As with traditional group experimental studies, the intent is to ensure that changes in responses (that is, in the dependent variables) are indeed the result of that intervention and are not a consequence of chance or other factors. Unlike most group-comparison experiments, however, a basic tenet is that decisions about results are made by expressly delineating what has occurred with each individual in the investigation.

Single-subject experimental research began in the 1950s with psychological studies exploring the aftermath of treatments with patients. There had been dissatisfaction among certain researchers when inferences from group investigations contrasted with influences of therapies actually seen or not seen with individual clients. Research designs were proposed that would allow therapists to measure changes in behavior for particular persons, singly. Although case-study research aimed at single individuals can disclose important trends, it does not allow unambiguous statements of cause and effect. It was intended that the new designs would have the capability of establishing functional and causal relationships, as can be done with group experimental procedures.

These single-subject experimental designs have evolved over the past few decades to allow analysis of many types of questions under many different circumstances. The most common designs are reversal designs, multiple-baseline designs, and alternating-treatments designs (also called multi-element designs), and each of these has variations. The characteristics of these designs and how they are used to demonstrate experimental control are described in Chapters 2, 3, and 4. Regardless of design type, however, most single-subject experimental studies follow certain basic procedures:

1. Baseline data, established through multiple measurement sessions, are collected before an intervention.

2. Variables are manipulated, and data are gathered frequently and over time throughout the intervention, and sometimes after.

3. Control procedures—rather than control groups—are used.

4. Standard measurement approaches are employed that examine permanent products or use observational recording.

5. Interobserver agreement for both the dependent and the independent variables are assessed.

6. All data are graphed.

7. Using specific guidelines, a visual—rather than a statistical—analysis is undertaken for each individual subject's graphed data. (Some single-subject researchers combine visual and statistical analyses—as described in Chapter 5—but many do not.)

8. Often maintenance data also are collected after the study proper, and sometimes transfer data are compiled. Both of the latter data types also are graphed.

9. The specific design selected allows for certain controls in interpreting the data so that conclusions are reliable and believable.

Use of single-subject experimental methodologies has expanded to several specialties within the field of psychology, and these designs are also now employed in medical studies, social work, investigations of communication disorders, and quite often special education. Though used less often in literacy work than are traditional group experiments and qualitative methods, single-subject experimental designs have been employed by some researchers—for example, to assess the results of reciprocal teaching on comprehension behaviors (Palincsar & Brown, 1983); to study the effects of teenage mothers on their children's literacy learning (Neuman & Gallagher, 1994); to evaluate a strategy for teaching students to identify multisyllabic words (Lenz & Hughes, 1990); to investigate the use of strategy training in improving students' skills in composing essays (Graham & Harris, 1989); to study teaching behaviors during concept instruction in content area classrooms (Bulgren, Schumaker, & Deshler, 1988); to examine the effects of meaning-focused cues on underachieving readers' context use and self-corrections (Mudre & McCormick, 1989); to assess story grammar instruction with high school students (Gurney, Gersten, Dimino, & Carnine, 1990); to investigate story-mapping training as a means of improving comprehension (Idol & Croll, 1987); to analyze the effects of study-skill programs on secondary students (Bianco & McCormick, 1989; McCormick & Cooper, 1991); and, in a teacher-research program, to compare the effectiveness of various assessment procedures for accurately evaluating students' word recognition (Braithwaite, 1987). The intent of this volume is to delineate the potential of single-subject experimental studies for other literacy educators and to describe the procedures one undertakes in such research.

Features of Single-Subject Experimental Research

Certain features of this research methodology make it unique. Some attributes seem similar to qualitative models for inquiry; others are more akin to patterns of analysis accompanying common group-investigation tactics.

Personalized Evaluation of Data

It is certainly true that group comparisons provide useful information for our field. However, in many traditional group research studies, after measuring individual responses and obtaining an average result by combining the responses of all group members, judgments about an intervention's merits often are based on this average. Therefore, significant information about specific individuals in a study can be obscured. In contrast, an important feature of single-subject experimental research is the personalization of data analysis. The goal is to demarcate each individual's current level or stage of responses at the beginning of an experiment and then to determine the degree to which approaches examined in the investigation change each individual's responses.

As acceptance of the single-subject experimental paradigm has spread and studies have proliferated, investigators have increasingly included several subjects within the same study—but still (with the exception of a few special circumstances discussed later) every participant's responses are analyzed individually. The term *single-subject research*, thus, refers to a process rather than to the actual number of participants. (If, for example, a study includes seven participants, data from these seven students, if analyzed appropriately, constitute seven complete experiments, or one experiment with six replications.)

Personalized analysis of data can provide important understandings about individual subjects as well as suggestions for the advancement of knowledge. Say, for example, that a group investigation includes fifth grade students who have literacy problems, and in that group there are pupils whose reading achievement ranges from approximately first grade level to third grade level. When postintervention behaviors are averaged we might find on the whole that an improvement has been shown, but, of course, inherent in any average are scores falling below and above that mean. Mean results do not tell us much about the effects of the treatment on specific pupils who are not represented by the mean. Unfortunately, too often findings are reported as general conclusions: "The *xyz* technique was effective with fifth grade disabled readers." But application of *xyz* to Susan, who had the lowest score in the group, or to others with learning levels and behaviors similar to Susan, may be quite ineffectual. A teacher using the *xyz* technique with Susan and her counterparts might be doing little to foster the learning of these children. Furthermore, a general conclusion that *xyz* is productive might close the books on the issue, with no further attempts made to tease out variations in the procedure that would allow learning for all.

This is not to say that group data can tell only about average response. Examination of standard deviations, for example, furnishes insights into variability in performance across a targeted group. But, although the research consumer can determine how much variation has occurred, seldom do traditional group analyses specify findings for specific individuals. It is true that some group designs have the potential for doing so; for example, in regression analysis after obtaining units for a population a researcher can use these to relate predictions to individuals. However, in regression analysis usually a relatively large number of subjects is needed.

In single-subject experimental research, on the other hand, even if there are only a few subjects, personalized as well as individual analysis is possible, is almost always undertaken, and is a major purpose of the research. At the conclusion of a study involving four subjects (say, Judy, Ricardo, Tanya, and John) the researcher will be able to specify exactly what has occurred with Judy in respect to her own unique responses before, during, and after an instructional intervention. The researcher can do the same for Ricardo—and for Tanya and John—and know the effects of the intervention personally for that individual. In some cases this may allow the investigator to conclude that an instructional intervention is effective for particular subjects in the study (perhaps Ricardo and John), but not for certain other specific subjects (Judy and Tanya).

Establishment of a Baseline

Just how is the process of individual data analysis played out in this methodology? One part of the goal is attained through gathering baseline data.

In group-comparison studies, data are typically obtained for two or more groups that have had contrasting treatments. If change is seen in one group and not in the others, this attests to the strength of a specific procedure, approach, method, policy, process, strategy, program, maneuver, technique, or the like. With single-subject experimental research, in many cases a student's changes in response are not contrasted with changes (or lack of changes) of other individuals in the study. And in almost all cases, changes are compared with the student's own preintervention level of responding. This is referred to as "using the subject as his or her own control," and is accomplished by collecting baseline data.

Baseline data are gathered for each subject during an initial phase of the research in which all conditions are carefully controlled so that they differ from the later phases in only one way: intervention procedures are absent. (Some designs also require a return to the baseline condition for a few sessions during the middle of the intervention; for example, see Yaden's description of reversal designs in Chapter 2.) Data gathered during the baseline period are displayed on a graph for later comparison with intervention data.

In single-subject experimental research, baseline information comprises more than a single pretest. Because human behaviors can show day-to-day variations, several opportunities are given for the student to exhibit his or her present (preintervention) level or stage of responding. The actual number of baseline-data–collection sessions can vary with the characteristics of the student being studied and with the research design. As is discussed in later chapters, when using certain single-subject designs the length of the baseline period changes even during different stages of the investigation. Although there are slight differences of opinion, a general rule of thumb suggested for most studies is that there be a minimum of five sessions or opportunities for a student to display preintervention behaviors. However, more than this minimum level may be needed because data collection in the baseline period often must continue until a stable trend is seen in the data (see the section on Establishment of Data Stability, following).

Figure 1.1 illustrates a typical graph for displaying baseline and intervention data when employing the often-used multiple-baseline design (see Chapter 3 for a complete description of this single-subject design, and Appendix A for a discussion of conventions used in preparing graphs). The graph, developed for a third grade nonreader named Thomas, was employed in a study investigating the effects of a procedure for increasing word learning (McCormick, 1991). During the investigation attempts were made to teach Thomas words from two books. The graph in this figure focuses on Book 1. Words from the book were divided into 4 sets of 10 words each, with each set assigned to a separate "tier," or axis, of the graph. The numerals 1 through 10 on the vertical axis of the graph, for each tier, represent the 10 words in each set. The numbers at the bottom of the graph on the horizontal axis indicate the trial or session in which Thomas demonstrated his knowledge of these words. When we look at his responses to the words in set 1 of Book 1, we can see from the data points that during the first baseline trial Thomas recognized no words, during the second trial he responded correctly to one word, during the third trial he knew no words, and on trials four and five he again correctly recognized a word. Though level in responding was low on all occasions during the baseline phase, there was slight variation from session to session (and for word sets 2, 3, and 4 displayed in the other tiers, there was even greater diversity from day to day). Examination of the figure shows that for all four sets of words his response on the first day of baseline-data collection was lower than what appears to be his most consistent level of recognition. Had that first day of baseline been the only instance of data collection before beginning intervention, a slightly inaccurate conclusion would have been drawn for later comparisons of his pre- and postintervention word knowledge. (Thomas's intervention data, also displayed on this graph, are discussed in the following section.)

Repeated Measurement Throughout the Intervention

Another distinguishing feature of single-subject experimental research is the repeated and frequent measurement of responses throughout intervention. Just as baseline information is not predicated on a single pretest, so too are intervention data appraised through more than a sole posttest. The

Figure 1.1
A Multiple-Baseline Graph

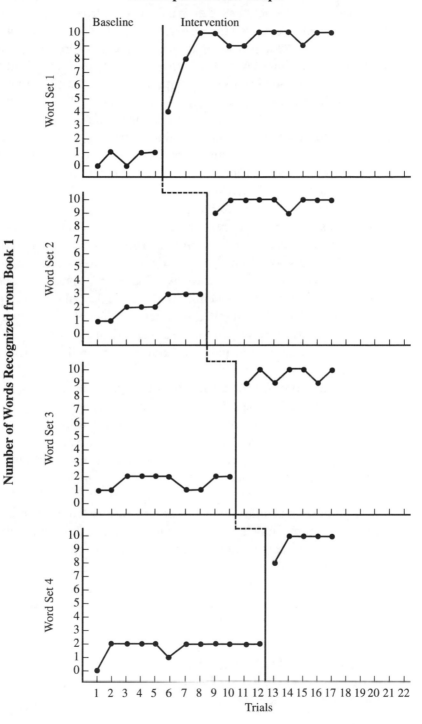

Number of Words Recognized from Book 1

logic is the same: day-to-day human variability may lead to faulty conclusions if decisions are based on responses made on one occasion alone. In single-subject studies, deductions are drawn from a pattern of behavior. Repeated measurement also allows the researcher to note response levels on specific trials when they appear to be atypically higher or lower than the general and most prevalent level of response. Not only does this limit erroneous inferences, it also permits examination of conditions during which different behaviors are seen, and thus may furnish critical insights for evaluating the intervention and for conducting later instruction.

Returning to Figure 1.1, we can see that numerous data points have been entered on Thomas's graph during the intervention phase; each point represents a measurement session. The first tier of the graph shows there was an immediate but small increase in his recognition of the words from the first set when the instructional strategy was introduced. By the third and fourth days of instruction he was recognizing all words in the first set correctly, but this pattern did not hold. He remained unsure of one word during the eight remaining sessions, sometimes recognizing it and sometimes not. Although his overall level of recognition was highly improved over baseline responses, there was some variability from day to day. In this example the variations are relatively insignificant, but this is not always the case. Recognition of the existence of periodic changes in behaviors is crucial to the integrity of research reports and to accurate understanding of instructional variables.

Repeated measurement also supplies other information. In the research design used with Thomas we can see from the graph that recognition of targeted words occurred more quickly in the second, third, and fourth sets than in the first. Thus, transfer of the instructed strategies seems apparent when we contrast the data points across the sets during intervention, as well as with data points during baseline—useful information to know.

The requirement in single-subject research for repeated measurement over time, as with case study and other qualitative research, frequently results in investigations that may occur over a prolonged period. In these studies the researcher cannot administer a pretest, apply an intervention for a few days, administer a posttest, and get out. Reasonably long-term commitments are often necessary, but the quality of the results can make the time expenditure worthwhile.

Establishment of Data Stability

Immediately after each measurement session, results are plotted on graphs for each subject. Rather than delaying the graphing of the data until later in the study or until the end, the researcher must graph immediately so he or she can make judgments about what must be done next.

With most of the designs used in single-subject experimental research (but not all—see Chapter 4 of this volume, for example), it is inappropriate to move from one condition to the next (for example, from baseline to intervention) until the subject's performance is stable in the present condition. Stability is assumed when a student's data show a similar level of responding across several measurement sessions. Whether the measurement is conducted during baseline or during intervention, a general policy sometimes used is that stability exists if approximately 85 percent (range = 80 percent–90 percent) of the data during a phase are within a 15 percent range of the average of all data points during that phase (Tawney & Gast, 1984). However, there are no hard and fast rules if exceptions can be justified. Recognizing the need for some flexibility in applied research, Heward (1987), for example, simply defines evidence of stability as existing when data points fall within a "narrow range."

Baseline data must be stable so the researcher can be reasonably sure that they represent a reliable picture of what the student would normally do without the presence of the intervention. Stable responding is the basis for accurate judgments when preintervention performance is compared with performances during and after intervention. The baseline portions of Figure 1.1 show that Thomas's responding was stable since there is similarity in response level across the baseline sessions; this is true in all four tiers of his graph.

On the other hand, a highly variable baseline would not allow such assurances. *Variability*, in these cases, is defined as the degree to which an individual's responses vary from time to time under the same experimental condition. This is often called *intrasubject variability*—that is, variability within an individual subject. Figure 1.2 exhibits an unstable baseline for a hypothetical subject during measurement sessions 1 to 5. When an unstable level of responding occurs, the researcher continues data collection in that condition until stability is achieved, before moving ahead to the next phase of the study. In Figure 1.2, the student's baseline data stabilize in sessions 6 through 9 and the researcher then institutes the intervention phase.

Stability of data during intervention conditions also is important in some designs if any reasonable conclusions are to be drawn—for instance, before moving back to a baseline condition when using a reversal design (see Chapter 2 of this volume) or before concluding the experiment as a whole.

An overall principle in single-subject studies is that the more data points that can be shown within each condition (baseline and interven-

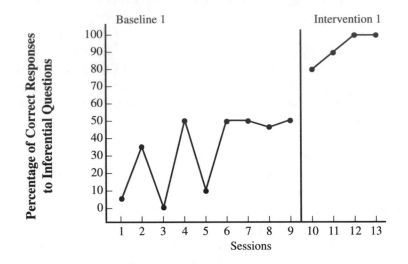

Figure 1.2
Graph Showing Early Nonstable Baseline Data

tion), the more believable the conclusions. However, the actual number needed depends to a large extent on the variability of the data. The more stable the responses, the fewer the number of data points needed in that condition; the more variable the responses, the greater the number of data points necessary.

The trend of the data also must be considered when making judgments about data stability. It is conventionally accepted that evidence of a trend exists when there are three consecutive data points in the same direction (Barlow & Hersen, 1984). This direction can show the data points moving upward (an increasing trend), moving downward (a decreasing trend), or on a flat plane. In Figure 1.3, (A) shows an increasing trend in the data on days 3, 4, and 5; (B) shows a decreasing trend on days 4, 5, and 6; and (C) illustrates a data trend on a flat plane in days 2, 3, and 4. At times, the researcher may hope that the data will ultimately move in an upward direction during intervention (showing, for example, an increase in correct responses to higher order questions). At other times, the desired direction when the intervention is applied is downward (showing, perhaps, a decrease in miscues during oral reading).

An increasing or decreasing trend during baseline data collection, however, is problematic. Increasing or decreasing trends during baseline indicate changes in responses without the application of the intervention. If these trends are already moving in the desired direction during the base-

McCormick

line condition, institution of the intervention may be unnecessary. And experimentally, no functional relationship could be shown between the independent variable of the intervention and the data obtained during that phase of the study.

A *functional relationship* is a quasi-causative relationship demonstrated when there are systematic changes in a dependent variable (that is, the data) as a result of introduction of the independent variable (that is, the intervention) (Baer, Wolf, & Risley, 1968). A functional relationship cannot be shown to exist if the subject's responses were already changing in the desired direction before the intervention procedures were begun. In some such cases, continuing baseline data collection may allow a stable level of response to emerge that is indicative of the student's most typical behavior; in other cases, a reevaluation of the need for the intervention is implied. Other requisites for establishing a functional relationship are discussed later. (Although one experiment may be sufficient to establish a possible functional relationship between an independent variable and the dependent vari-

Figure 1.3
Graphs Showing Increasing, Decreasing, and Flat-Plane Data Trends

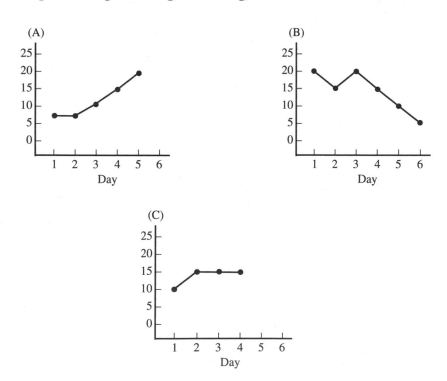

able, it is often assumed that several replications are needed to show a cause-and-effect relationship. A conservative posture adopted by many researchers is that no one experiment, no matter the method used, should result in general assumptions of cause and effect. This view is held by most single-subject researchers. On this subject, see, for example, Johnston and Pennypacker, 1993.)

Manipulation of Variables

As in group experiments, in single-subject experimental studies there is direct manipulation of variables. This is not research in which the investigator focuses exclusively on existing conditions. Investigations are devised to observe if there is change (or lack of change) in behavior with respect to specifically planned procedures; deductions are not built ex post facto.

In most cases only one procedure is examined at a time. This enables researchers to determine the impact of specific variables on the observed outcomes. Though many experiments include multiple elements, designs can be selected to allow each to be appraised separately. An example is seen in Figure 1.4. This graph displays data obtained using an alternating-treatments design in a study of five adult low-proficiency readers in which the focus of instruction was on increasing knowledge of word meanings (Mullins, 1989). Three instructional conditions were examined to assess their relative effects on learning and transfer. As can be seen on the graph, each condition was applied and measured in different sessions. For example, the study was initiated in session 1 with an application of instructional condition I; in session 2, instructional condition III was applied; in session 3, condition II was instituted; in session 4, condition III was used again; and so on. (More about alternating-treatments designs can be learned in Chapter 4.)

Standard Measurement Procedures

In single-subject experiments, procedures for measuring the effects of variables are designated before instituting any data collection and are constant throughout every condition of the investigation—in baseline, during intervention, and during measurement of maintenance and transfer.

Most measurement processes are the same as those routinely used in other literacy studies. For example, measurement may be grounded on *permanent* (or *lasting*) *products* obtained from responses that result in material items or lasting effects that researchers can evaluate at a later time, rather than as they happen. Such items might include scores from formal and informal tests, writing samples, audiotapes of oral reading, and videotapes

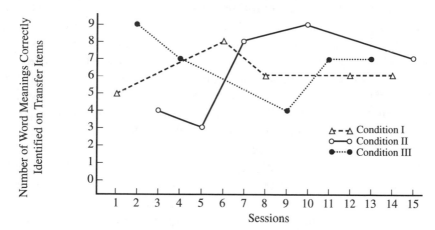

Figure 1.4
Graph Showing Three Conditions Applied and Measured Separately

Note: From *An analysis of the effects of three procedures for increasing word knowledge of older disabled readers*, by N. Mullins, 1989, unpublished doctoral dissertation, the Ohio State University, Columbus. Reprinted with permission of the author.

of interactions during literature circles. Permanent products allow the researcher to develop accurate and reliable analyses after the fact.

Observational recording also may be used. If the investigator is interested in an important function that does not produce a permanent product or if using equipment to record pupils' actions would disrupt naturally occurring behaviors, then he or she may watch and record behaviors as they transpire. To do so, single-subject researchers often use these types of observational data collection: event recording, interval recording, momentary time sampling, duration recording, and latency recording (Cooper, 1987).

Event recording simply involves observing the times an operation or response happens and counting it. An example is recording the number of oral responses a pupil makes during cooperative-learning activities versus the number made in teacher-led groups.

If the acts of interest to the investigator are expected to occur at a high rate, *interval recording* may be substituted for event recording. To do this, the experimenter divides the observation period into short intervals and records the occurrence of the action if it is displayed any time within that interval. *Momentary time sampling* is used similarly. The observation time is broken into equal increments and a notation is made if the behavior was occurring at the moment the interval ends.

Duration recording can be used when the researcher is interested in how long a student engages in an activity. The researcher can measure "total duration"—that is, the total time during an observation period that a student is actively engaged in a behavior (for example, amount of time spent in writing after a story has been read versus writing when no literary stimulus precedes the task). Measures of "duration per occurrence" can also be taken—that is, the researcher notes the duration of several displays of the targeted behavior in any given observation period. For example, if during class periods of sustained silent reading, Andrea engages in reading only now and then, the length of time she sustains reading during each of her engagements with text might be recorded.

Latency recording entails measuring the amount of time that elapses between a stimulus and a response. Word recognition research, for instance, is concerned not only with accuracy and automaticity but also with how quickly a student recognizes words. Latency measures also can be used in fluency studies.

Needless to say, the quality of the measurement procedures—including verification of the validity, accuracy, and reliability of the measurements—is crucial to generating usable results.

Assessment of Maintenance

A fairly routine policy of single-subject experimental research is the inclusion of maintenance measures. Typically, the researcher returns to the participant or participants one month after termination of the study, with no direct intervention in the meantime. The researcher then reevaluates the students' responses using the same or comparable measures as employed earlier to determine if improvements seen during the intervention have been maintained.

The criticality of maintaining learning hardly needs to be discussed. Quite obviously it does little good for pupils to exhibit improved levels of understanding only until the end of a research investigation. Though literacy researchers have been urged to incorporate maintenance assessments in their studies, they have not always done so. Many single-subject researchers hold that a study is incomplete until an appraisal of maintenance of the learned behaviors has been accomplished.

Evaluation of Transfer

Transfer of knowledge and strategies to other contexts also is crucial in order for learning to advance, and evaluation of transfer is important for planning solid research that offers productive insights for the literacy field. For example, after measuring student responses during teacher-directed instruction as a result of a planned intervention, one might evaluate the responses under independent reading conditions; after collecting data on use of an instructed metacognitive strategy while students are reading material on a familiar topic, one might collect data on its use when the subjects are reading about unfamiliar topics. Like maintenance evaluations, however, transfer measures have not always been included in research in our field.

Though it is somewhat less characteristic than including maintenance assessment, single-subject researchers have embraced the notion of evaluating transfer somewhat more ardently than we in literacy research traditionally have. A fairly standard feature of published reports of single-subject experimental investigations is a description of procedures and outcomes related to transfer of the targeted understandings.

Substantiation of Internal Validity

Internal validity refers to the degree to which findings of an experiment can be ascribed to the intervention and not to faults in the study's methodology. Because subjects serve as their own controls, many standard threats to the internal validity of an investigation (such as differential selection that leads to the nonequivalence of an experimental group and a control group) present a lesser problem in single-subject research than in some other experimental paradigms. Furthermore, as you will see in later chapters, the standard designs used as a part of this methodology are specifically arranged to account for many common concerns of internal validity. Researchers employing these methodologies also build into their studies procedures for assessing interobserver agreement for the dependent variables and for assessing the integrity of the independent variable. The former is routine in most sound inquiry, whatever the paradigm. The latter, though frequently recommended, often has been ignored in studies couched within other methodological models.

To evaluate interobserver agreement for the dependent variable, trained observers, raters, or judges select a percentage of the data and reappraise it. Percentages of agreement are reported, a typical policy with competently conducted group-comparison investigations as well. Analogous procedures are seen in qualitative studies in the use of multiple data sources, triangulation, and other strategies designed to heighten the believability of conclusions.

Assessment of the integrity of the independent variable—also called substantiation of treatment reliability or a manipulation check (Pressley, Lysynchuk, D'Ailly, Smith, & Cake, 1989)—assures the research consumer that the results communicated in a research report are related to the intervention procedures as specifically delineated in that report. This is important, because if the researcher has drifted from the planned procedures during the conduct of the study, then one cannot attribute the responses obtained to the intervention as described. Likewise, if subjects did not carry out the procedures in the way they were directed to—that is, the procedures as specified in the report of the study—other alternative causes for the response changes cannot be ruled out.

To judge the integrity of the independent variable in single-subject experimental research, interventions are preplanned by the experimenter and then, during the study, monitored by an observer. To do this, specifications of all procedures are delineated by the researcher prior to initiating data collection, usually by listing steps and precisely spelling out the parameters of techniques to be employed. These are placed on a checklist to be used by the observer. (See Figure 1.5 for a sample observer's checklist.) The observer then randomly selects a percentage of both the baseline and instructional sessions to observe, and during these observations compares what is seen with the list of steps and parameters, noting the degree to which the planned procedures are followed. A percentage of consistency of implementation is determined by dividing the total number of instances when any procedural step was not followed during the observation by the total number of opportunities to follow all procedural steps during the session. This percentage of the consistency of implementation is stated in the research report.

In general, single-subject experimental research is robust in regard to internal validity. However, this does not mean that there are no considerations in this area that must be taken into account. Further aspects of this issue are explored by Palincsar and Parecki in Chapter 8.

Analysis of Visual Data

In single-subject experimental research, conclusions about the worth of an intervention are based on visual inspection of the data displayed on the graphs maintained throughout the study. At times visual analysis is joined with a statistical analysis, but more often it is not. Whether to employ a supplementary statistical analysis has been a point of controversy among single-subject researchers. Some argue strongly about the limitations of statistical analyses and others point to the advantages that statistical applications add to visual analysis. In Chapter 5, Kamil provides some insights that can be considered in this debate.

Visual analysis is valued by single-subject investigators for making sense of research results for several reasons:

1. Graphed data allow an ongoing view of student performance as the study progresses.

McCormick

Figure 1.5
Sample Observer's Checklist

Intervention Phase
(Observation of Instruction and Measurement)

Observer _____ Session No. _____ Date _____

	Yes	No
1. To introduce the lesson, researcher used the prereading questions previously prepared for today's story.		

1. To introduce the lesson, researcher used the prereading questions previously prepared for today's story.

2. Researcher used all of the previously prepared questions.

3. Researcher did not use questions other than those previously prepared.

4. Researcher attempted to involve all students in oral discussion of answers to the questions.

5. After group participation in answering each of the three background questions, students wrote their own individual responses to one of the questions.

6. After group participation in answering each of the three prediction questions, students wrote their own individual responses to one of the questions.

7. Researcher told students (in some fashion) that "Whenever we read we should think about what we already know about the subject to help us understand the information we're reading."

8. Researcher had students listen to the read-along side of the audiotape for today's story.

9. Students had copies of story to follow and they each read silently as they listened to the tape.

10. Group reread story orally, volunteering for turns.

11. All students participated in the oral reading activity.

12. Researcher orally asked three previously prepared inferential questions after students read story.

13. Researcher asked no other oral questions after the story.

14. Researcher attempted to involve all students in oral responding to questions asked after story was read.

15. Researcher helped students relate oral questions and answers discussed after the story to their own background experiences.

16. Researcher helped students relate oral questions and answers discussed after the story to their prereading predictions.

17. Students answered three additional written questions that called for inferences, doing so independently.

18. Researcher told students words that they had difficulty reading in the written questions, if they asked.

19. Researcher did not give help with spelling or provide any other clues to the answers to the written questions.

- -
Comments:

What Is Single-Subject Research?   17

2. Throughout the study and at its end the researcher can consider what has occurred in each and all measurement sessions, and thus, variability in responses can be assessed for each individual.

3. Visual analysis of graphed data does not specify preset levels of significance that must be obtained to judge the effectiveness of interventions. The researcher therefore makes decisions about the educational significance, rather than the statistical significance, of the results.

4. Conclusions about an intervention's merits can be drawn relatively quickly.

5. Visual analysis presents a conservative view of data because findings that might demonstrate statistical significance may not be interpreted as strong and stable when the complete array of the graphic display is appraised (Heward, 1987; Parsonson & Baer, 1978).

The heart of the visual analysis consists of comparing the data points on the graph displaying baseline behaviors with the data points indicating intervention behaviors (as seen in Figure 1.1), or comparing the data points displaying behaviors during different interventions (as seen in Figure 1.4). (Data exhibited for maintenance and transfer conditions are compared with both baseline and intervention data points.) In most cases the researcher examines these data to see (1) if a change has occurred, (2) the magnitude of the change, (3) the trend of the change, (4) the latency of the change, and (5) if the change appears reliable.

Determining if a change has occurred. To determine whether a change has occurred, the investigator examines the level of the data points in each condition and makes a comparison between conditions. Although the overall mean level of response in each condition may be considered in this comparison, variability of response also must be taken into account, since consideration of means alone can at times obscure the true nature of the data. For example, in Figure 1.6, the dotted horizontal lines, called "mean level lines," show that the mean level of response during the intervention phase is slightly higher than that during the first baseline phase. However, as can be seen, while level of responding during this intervention condition increased over baseline levels in half of the sessions, it actually decreased in the other half—not a particularly productive result.

Furthermore, at times data points may "overlap" between conditions—that is, the subject's response levels during certain measurement sessions in one condition may be the same as those in measurement sessions in a different condition. In Figure 1.7 for instance, in (A) the data points for sessions 2 and 4 during an initial baseline phase represent the

Figure 1.6

Figure 1.6
Graph Showing Mean Level of Response Versus Variability of Response

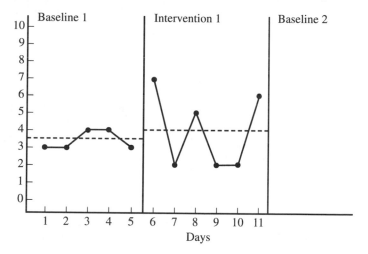

Note: Mean level of response for Baseline 1 data = 3.4; meal level for intervention data = 4.0.

same level of responding as data points during a first intervention phase in sessions 7, 9, and 12. At other times, as illustrated in (B), no data in one condition fall within the range of the data points displayed in another condition. It is when this occurs that the strongest argument can be made that there is a difference between the conditions. The more the overlap, the less strength there is in such a conclusion.

Determining the magnitude of a change. Although it is relatively easy to decide whether a change has occurred, questions of magnitude are more complex. One can readily determine the quantitative aspects of magnitude by observing the number (or percentage or the like) of desired responses in varying conditions. However, the qualitative aspect of magnitude must also be evaluated. Rather than asking if there is a statistically significant difference between conditions, more often single-subject researchers ask if the difference is educationally significant. If Jim typically can answer 3 of 10 inferential questions correctly under the baseline condition and consistently answers 5 of 10 correctly under the intervention condition, is that an educationally significant difference? Such judgments must be made in light of the individual student, the specific situation, and the particular research question. On the one hand, we might be pleased with Jim's consistently improved results, but on the other hand, he still shows difficulties with half the questions. Thus, the researcher must not only note the distance be-

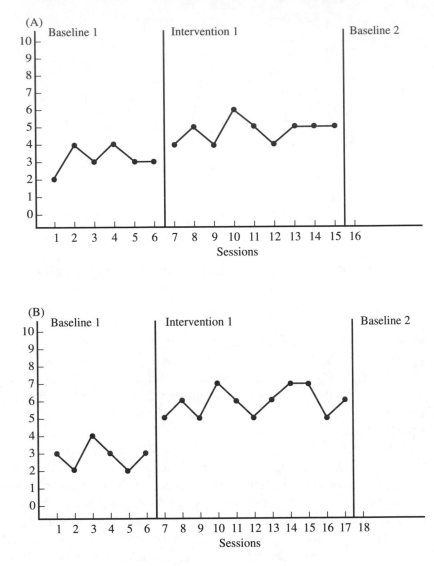

Figure 1.7
Graphs Showing Overlap and Lack of Overlap of Data Points

tween data lines but must also exercise judgment about the meaningfulness of that distance in specific circumstances.

Determining the trend of a change. Asking about the trend of a change addresses the question of whether the differences are in the right direction. The purpose of a research investigation determines whether an increasing or decreasing trend in the data as a result of the intervention is hoped for.

We would not be pleased to see an intervention that produced fewer coveted responses than were present without the intervention! Furthermore, we hope that maintenance measures reveal no change or a continually improving trend from positive intervention data.

Determining the latency of a change. To consider latency is to question how long it takes to see a change in response. The researcher asks, "Is change immediate? Does it occur after a few applications of the intervention? Does it occur after prolonged applications of the intervention? Does it occur more quickly with one intervention than with another?"

Determining the reliability of a change. Asking how reliable a change is brings into play again the issue of data stability. The researcher examines the graphs to determine whether the changed responses are consistently and dependably displayed, and whether they are maintained over time. This examination concerns not only data within the initial baseline condition or a single intervention condition, but depends to a large extent on examining data across like conditions. Repeating the same phases within a single experiment is important for addressing the question of whether changes in responses are reliable. Each of the major designs used in single-subject research has built into its framework a specific manner for allowing repetitions of each specific condition. In Figure 1.1, for example, you can see four replications of the baseline condition and four replications of the intervention phase within a multiple-baseline design. In a reversal design (see Figure 1.8), conditions may be alternated between baseline and intervention phases two or more times—for instance, beginning with a baseline phase, instituting the intervention, returning to the baseline phase, and then reinstituting the intervention.

The term *direct replication* is used to refer to this repetition of phases within a single experiment. A different type of direct replication that would furnish additional information about how reliable a result is might involve repeating the same experiment with the same subject or subjects, but in a different setting—perhaps the original study was conducted in a clinic and the direct replication in a classroom—or with the same subject(s) in different contexts—perhaps measuring a student's comprehension as a result of the same instructional procedures applied to narratives and also to exposition. Repeated observation and measurement of the same subject or subjects is also called *intrasubject* (or *intraindividual*) *replication*, and can occur in the same experiment or in different experiments.

Line graphs. Most often line graphs are employed to display the data used in all these visual analyses. Certain conventions have been adopted for preparing graphs in order to aid interpretation across research reports. Appendix A of this volume delineates major points to consider in preparing

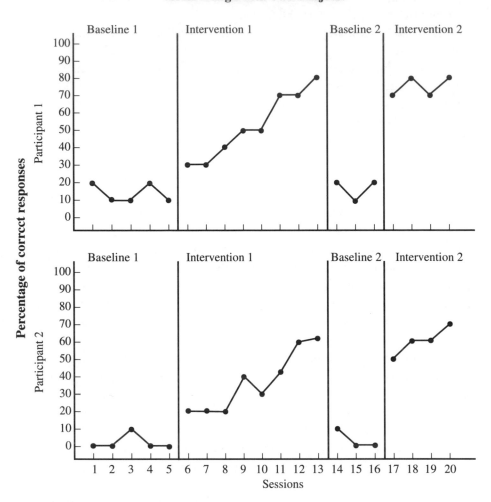

graphs for single-subject studies. Additional information can be found in Heward (1987) and in Tawney and Gast (1984).

Establishment of External Validity

As in qualitative studies, the most controversial aspect of single-subject research is the matter of *external validity*. External validity pertains to generalizability. How can we know if results with one subject, or only a few subjects, apply to others? As with judgments of reliability, the single-subject experimenter bases statements of generalizability on replication.

In group-comparison research, generality of effects is assumed when large numbers of subjects are studied and, most important, when they are randomly selected and/or randomly assigned to treatment conditions. While it is a widely accepted axiom that the results obtained from such a study will be relevant for students sharing the same characteristics, some have argued that for participants in a research investigation to be genuinely representative of a larger unstudied group, they must share a *great number* of characteristics with that group (see Sidman, 1960). Even with a sizable number of subjects and stratified sampling methods, this is still a complex requirement.

The tactic taken by single-subject researchers to establish generality is to use direct as well as systematic replication. Direct replication to assess reliability (as described earlier) is undertaken with the same subjects. However, when one wishes to answer questions of generalizability, direct replication consists of the same experiment with different subjects who have characteristics similar to those in the original group (Barlow & Hersen, 1984). Generalizability can also be assessed through systematic replication, which is usually conducted after a series of direct replication studies in which the intervention has proved to be successful. In systematic replications the same experiment is carried out with subjects who are less similar than or not similar to the previous subjects to further appraise the extent of the generality of the findings. Systematic replications also may be conducted in different settings and contexts.

Intersubject (or *interindividual*) *replication* refers to the repetition of the same experiment with different subjects. Although this can be undertaken in different investigations (as just described), in fact, any single-subject study that includes more than one participant constitutes a type of intersubject replication.

Generality is assumed if the findings are the same after a body of replications. The number of replications required for generality to be accepted depends on the intricacy of the research question, the size of the effect in each replication, and the obviousness of the results, among other considerations.

At times the question of generalizing results is not of great importance. For instance, in certain cases the research may be concerned only with the needs of a specific pupil or a small group (for example, see Chapter 7 of this volume).

Additional issues related to achieving external validity in single-subject experimental research are addressed by Palincsar and Parecki in Chapter 8.

Cautious Generation of Group Comparisons

The purpose for which single-subject experimental research methodologies were developed was to obtain the refined data allowed by personalized analysis. Even though there may be several participants in a study, these advantages are realized by examining and by reporting each participant's data individually. However, occasionally the procedures ascribed to this paradigm are applied to the combined data of groups. At times this is done for appropriate reasons, but at other times it is not.

Acceptable instances. Some questions asked by literacy researchers inherently involve interactions among participants in a study, interactions that come into play in the responses obtained. An example is seen in an investigation of writing behaviors reported by Danoff, Harris, and Graham (1993). These researchers wanted to know the effects on students' writing created during a writing workshop that employed student dyads working together. The instructional model stressed active collaboration and interactive learning between the students in each pair. Danoff et al. adapted the individual-subject analysis tactics of the basic multiple-baseline design (see Chapter 3 of this volume) to examine and report their data through a multiple-baseline-across-pairs-of-subjects design. Data were graphed for each dyad instead of for each participant.

Johnston and Pennypacker (1993) suggest that sometimes one might want to study the effects of a well-established program on solving the problems of a particular group. For example, a method for promoting some aspect of students' literacy learning may already have been shown to be effective through previous replications in single-subject research (or through traditional group studies) with a large enough number of students who share characteristics with a new targeted group. In this case, the question is less one of determining program effectiveness and more one of verifying that this accepted program is effective with a certain specific group. This may be the case particularly in applied research in schools. For example, Mr. Brown, a program supervisor, may think that the Super-Duper Method will facilitate learning in the middle school learning disabilities classes in his school district, but rather than guessing and hoping, he collects data for classroom groups in each school to see if Super-Duper works for them. Thus, if the research question does not involve studying the program, method, or procedure itself, then group data might be sufficient to demonstrate an improvement for a set of individuals. Johnston and Pennypacker point out, however, that if the collated group responses do not show the hoped for trend, then a problem exists: when composite group data collected through single-subject experimental methods are all that are available, one does not know how many and which individuals are failing to respond to the intervention. In Mr. Brown's case, for example, it is possible that a few unusually unresponsive students might mask the productiveness of the method for the majority of a class.

In addition, group data can be reported to summarize individual data, with the individual data also collected, analyzed, and displayed. For example, in their research report, Smith and Jones may include graphs for each of the six participants in their study of metacognitive strategy use and in addition provide a group graph that aggregates the data and furnishes a quick look at the overall results. A group graph is considered only supplemental to the individual graphs, however, and should not be used if the averaged data do not represent a very close approximation of what can be seen in the individually displayed responses. Figure 1.9, for instance, is an example in which the averaged data do not look like the data for any single individual in the study. Graph (s1) for Subject 1 shows, in the first condition, a sharply increasing trend in the data; (s2) for Subject 2 displays a sharply decreasing trend; (s3) for Subject 3 shows a low level of response; and (s4) for Subject 4 displays a much higher response level. When these data for the first condition are averaged, as shown in the top graph in the figure, the line representing this average does not depict the response behavior of any of the four subjects. This also is true for the data in the second condition illustrated in these graphs.

Unacceptable instances. In high-quality single-subject research, examining group data instead of conducting individual analyses simply for purposes of expediency is not condoned. As Johnston and Pennypacker (1993) point out, defining the subject as the group restrains the interpretations permitted by the ensuing data—that is, one then cannot generate inferences about the outcomes of the intervention on the learning of any specific individual. They state, "Grouped measures of individual behavior inevitably lose contact with the defining features of each member's behavior, and we must restrict our interpretations accordingly" (p. 82).

If the question being asked in a literacy study does not seem to require personalized data analysis, it often is wiser to select analysis procedures from the traditional group methodological paradigm. Data collection is usually quicker with such procedures, and they may offer some advantages that are not commonly found in single-subject experimental research. One example is the provision of standard deviations to lead to accurate conclusions about group data.

Experimental Logic

All of the features of single-subject research reflect an experimental logic basic to this paradigm that is predicated on three major components: prediction, verification, and replication.

Figure 1.9
Graphs Showing an Instance Where Group Data Are Not
Representative of Individual Data

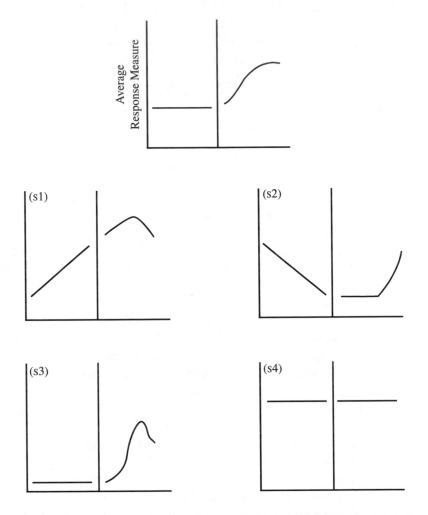

Note: From *Strategies and Tactics of Behavioral Research* (p. 305), by J.M. Johnston and H.S. Penny-packer, 1993, Hillsdale, NJ: Erlbaum. Copyright 1993; reprinted with permission.

McCormick

Prediction is satisfied through adherence to the guideline that specifies measurement of baseline data until a stable level of responding is seen. In other words, if a student shows a consistent level of response over a period of time, one can predict that his or her response level would continue to fall within that range if no intervention was instituted. Stable baseline data predict future behavior and are the foundation on which single-subject evaluation is grounded. Similarly, prediction is important in intervention phases. Measurement is repeated in any given intervention condition until it is apparent that the pattern of data points indicates what the student would normally continue to do under the condition. Obviously, regardless of whether the measurements are taken in a baseline or intervention phase, the greater the consistency in level or rate of responding over a number of measurement sessions, the stronger the predictive power.

Verification is the second basic element in the experimental logic of single-subject research. If the researcher predicts that response levels seen in baseline will not change without the introduction of the intervention and they do not, and then he or she predicts that they will change with the introduction of this intervention and they do, this confirms the predictions the researcher has made. It is not yet possible to assume a functional relationship, however, because variables unrelated to the intervention may be responsible for the change.

Verification refers to a requirement that the researcher must show, in some way, that the baseline range of responding would indeed have stayed the same if this intervention had not been carried out (Risley & Wolf, 1972). This is the first step in determining whether a functional relationship exists. Verification is established somewhat differently in each of the designs commonly used in single-subject experimental studies: in reversal designs by briefly returning to the baseline condition, in multiple-baseline designs by beginning interventions at different times for different subjects or responses, and by other procedures (described in depth in Chapters 2, 3, and 4). The procedures used for verification in these designs lessen, to a considerable degree, threats to internal validity—that is, the possibility that factors extraneous to the intervention were influential in bringing about the differences seen in the responses.

Replication within a single experiment is critical, as seen earlier, in serving as the basis for confirming reliability of results. Repeating like phases within experiments (as, for example, in the repetitions of the baseline condition and the intervention condition shown in Figure 1.8) not only confirms that response changes can be made to occur more than once and are therefore reliable, but also adds more assurances that the intervention, rather than extraneous variables, was decisive in these changes.

What Is Single-Subject Research?   27

Demonstrating evidence for predictions, verification of the predictions, and replications that show similar responses in like phases, together provide a strong case for a functional relationship between the intervention and the data obtained.

Conclusion

Although single-subject experimental research is helpful for answering a wide variety of literacy questions, it may be particularly useful for studying subjects in remedial programs. When the conclusions of group research are based on mean results, the widely differing learning characteristics, needs, aptitudes, and motivations of specific students may not be addressed. The personalized evaluation inherent in single-subject studies presents good possibilities for furnishing insights to refine our perceptions about delayed readers.

Use of single-subject experimental methods also provides a solution when it is unrealistic to administer procedures with sizable samples in one setting (such as experimentation with parents or studies with illiterate adults), or, relatedly, when large numbers of individuals are not readily available (for instance, clinical populations of a specific type). Pressley (personal communication, May 1994) suggests the applicability of these designs for investigations of rarely encountered disorders, such as research with students who have unusual brain anomalies or children who were born to drug-addicted mothers.

Furthermore, single-subject experimental investigations may serve as follow-ups to case-study research: the case-study data can document existing conditions, and the single-subject follow-up(s) can explore attempts to bring about changes in those conditions, if a need for change is indicated. Clinical case studies often go beyond observations of present conditions by instituting interventions. The in-depth observations in this type of case study are undertaken to judge the differences seen (or not seen) with a single individual as a result of a procedure that is applied. A study or studies then can follow, employing single-subject experimental methodology to substantiate functional relationships among variables or, with the use of replications, to establish cause and effect. An example of the latter is seen in a series of ongoing studies with severely disabled readers. In the first, a longitudinal case study examined the effects of a specific instructional technique in helping an older seriously delayed reader to enter the earliest stages of literacy acquisition (McCormick, 1994). In subsequent studies, single-subject experimental investigations have been used with the same instructional method but different subjects to answer the functional relationship and cause-effect questions (see, for example, McCormick, 1991). Bisesi and Raphael furnish additional suggestions for combining qualitative and single-subject experimental procedures in Chapter 6 of this volume.

Single-subject research may also serve as a forerunner to traditional group research. An often-suggested application of single-subject experimental studies is to lay the groundwork by formulating hypotheses that later may be verified or disconfirmed through group methods.

Researchers also may consider using single-subject studies because of their relative efficiency. Repeatedly obtaining the same results with several different subjects across a single experiment (intra-experiment direct replications), or with several participants across each of several experiments (interexperiment direct or systematic replications), can be as impressive as a large-group study in suggesting inferences and is more cost efficient in terms of number of subjects, and perhaps in terms of number of experimenters needed to execute the study (Pressley, personal communication, May 1994). This consideration must be balanced, though, by keeping in mind the potential long time span for data collection necessary in many single-subject investigations.

In addition, single-subject methodology is well suited for teacher research in schools since it can be situated in ongoing instruction. In fact, it is employed as an evaluation strategy in just that way in many special education programs. Data from these evaluations, collected by teachers in their classrooms with their students, influence choices about program planning for individuals and for overall curriculum design. Many features of single-subject research may also be attractive to those in the literacy field who direct or engage in program evaluations (such as teachers, program coordinators, supervisors, and administrators). Positive features of single-subject experimental investigations for teacher research and school-based evaluation include the personalized nature of the data; the recognition that students' responses vary from day to day; the use of measurement procedures natural to most classrooms (such as formal and informal test scores, writing samples, and observation); the concern for maintenance of learning; the use of subjects as their own controls, thus precluding the need for control groups; the ability to examine a teaching procedure in a specific context; the relative ease of analyzing the data, since statistical expertise is unnecessary; and the activist purpose of this paradigm to bring about change. This methodology provides practice-oriented ways for field-based personnel to learn more about what is effective—and what is not—in what they do. Braithwaite devotes all of Chapter 7 of this volume to examples of single-subject evaluation studies used by school-based educators.

Shannon (1991) points out that research modes furnish diverse ways to contemplate and understand. In addition to focusing on the varying assumptions and criteria for different analytical perspectives, it might be productive to explore ways that assorted methodologies can complement one another and answer different but equally important questions. See Appendix B for a general comparison of some of these methodologies.

Although they have gained popularity in such fields as educational psychology and learning disabilities as well as in other professions, single-subject experimental designs are not yet widely used in reading or writing research. The authors of this volume believe that the time is overdue for literacy investigators to consider single-subject experimental studies as viable options when attempting to answer certain types of instructional questions. The remaining chapters in this book provide detailed guidance for choosing and using various single-subject experimental procedures and designs in literacy research.

References

Baer, D.M., Wolf, M.M., & Risley, T.R. (1968). Some current dimensions of applied behavior analysis. *Journal of Applied Behavior Analysis, 1*, 91–97.

Barlow, D.H., & Hersen, M. (1984). *Single case experimental designs* (2nd ed.). New York: Pergamon.

Bianco, L., & McCormick, S. (1989). Analysis of effects of a reading study skill program for high school learning-disabled students. *Journal of Educational Research, 82*, 282–288.

Braithwaite, J.A. (1987). *The effectiveness of three assessment procedures to accurately predict disabled readers' word recognition.* Unpublished doctoral dissertation, Ohio State University, Columbus, OH.

Bulgren, J., Schumaker, J.B., & Deshler, D.D. (1988). Effectiveness of a concept teaching routine in enhancing the performance of LD students in secondary level mainstream classes. *Learning Disability Quarterly, 11*, 3–16.

Cooper, J.O. (1987). Measuring and recording behavior. In J.O. Cooper, T.E. Heron, & W.L. Heward (Eds.), *Applied behavior analysis* (pp. 59–80). Columbus, OH: Merrill.

Danoff, B., Harris, K.R., & Graham, S. (1993). Incorporating strategy instruction within the writing process in the regular classroom: Effects on the writing of students with and without learning disabilities. *Journal of Reading Behavior, 25*, 295–322.

Graham, S., & Harris, K.R. (1989). Improving learning disabled students' skills at composing essays: Self-instructional strategy training. *Exceptional Children, 56*, 201–214.

Gurney, D., Gersten, R., Dimino, J., & Carnine, D. (1990). Story grammar: Effective literature instruction for high school students with learning disabilities. *Journal of Learning Disabilities, 6*, 335–342, 348.

Heward, W.L. (1987). Production and interpretation of graphic data displays. In J.O. Cooper, T.E. Heron, & W.L. Heward (Eds.), *Applied behavior analysis* (pp. 106–141). Columbus, OH: Merrill.

Idol, L., & Croll, V.J. (1987). Story-mapping training as a means of improving reading comprehension. *Learning Disability Quarterly, 10*, 214–299.

Johnston, J.M., & Pennypacker, H.S. (1993). *Strategies and tactics of behavioral research* (2nd ed.). Hillsdale, NJ: Erlbaum.

Lenz, B.K., & Hughes, C.A. (1990). A word identification strategy for adolescents with learning disabilities. *Journal of Learning Disabilities, 23*, 149–158.

McCormick, S. (1991, December). *Working with our most severe reading disability cases: A strategy for teaching nonreaders*. Paper presented at the meeting of the National Reading Conference, Palm Springs, CA.

McCormick, S. (1994). A nonreader becomes a reader: A case study of literacy acquisition by a severely disabled reader. *Reading Research Quarterly, 29,* 156–177.

McCormick, S., & Cooper, J.O. (1991). Can sq3r facilitate secondary learning disabled students' literal comprehension of expository text? Three experiments. *Reading Psychology, 12,* 239–271.

Mudre, L.H., & McCormick, S. (1989). Effects of meaning-focused cues on underachieving readers' context use, self-corrections, and literal comprehension. *Reading Research Quarterly, 24,* 89–113.

Mullins, N. (1989). An analysis of the effects of three procedures for increasing word knowledge of older disabled readers (Doctoral dissertation, Ohio State University). *Dissertation Abstracts International, 50,* 911A.

Neuman, S.B., & Gallagher, P. (1994). Joining together in literacy learning: Teenage mothers and children. *Reading Research Quarterly, 29,* 383–401.

Palincsar, A.S. & Brown, A.L. (1983). *Reciprocal teaching of comprehension-fostering and comprehension-monitoring activities* (Tech. Rep. No. 269). Urbana–Champaign, IL: University of Illinois, Center for the Study of Reading.

Parsonson, B., & Baer, D.M. (1978). The analysis and presentation of graphic data. In T.R. Kratochwill (Ed.), *Single-subject research: Strategies for evaluating change* (pp. 101–167). New York: Academic.

Pressley, M., Lysynchuk, L.M., D'Ailly, H., Smith, M., & Cake, H. (1989). A methodological analysis of experimental studies of comprehension strategy instruction. *Reading Research Quarterly, 24,* 458–470.

Risley, T.R., & Wolf, M.M. (1972). Strategies for analyzing behavioral change over time. In J. Nesselroade & H. Reese (Eds.), *Life-span developmental psychology: Methodological issues* (pp. 175–183). New York: Academic.

Shannon, P. (1991). Politics, policy, and reading research. In R. Barr, M.L. Kamil, P. Mosenthal, & P.D. Pearson (Eds.), *Handbook of reading research: Volume II* (pp. 147–168). White Plains, NY: Longman.

Sidman, M. (1960). *Tactics of scientific research: Evaluating experimental data in psychology.* New York: Basic.

Tawney, J.W., & Gast, D.L. (1984). *Single-subject research in special education.* Columbus, OH: Merrill.

CHAPTER 2

Reversal Designs

David B. Yaden, Jr.

The purpose of this chapter is to introduce, describe, and suggest applications in literacy studies for reversal designs in single-subject experimental research. Considered by many to be the prototypical approach to experimentation in single-subject investigations (see, for example, Barlow & Hersen, 1984), this design and its many variants have been used extensively in clinical and experimental psychology during the past two decades and have had wide application in several fields of special education, including the areas of communication disorders (McReynolds & Thompson, 1986; Siegel & Young, 1987), deaf education (Bullis & Anderson, 1986; Luetke-Stahlman, 1986), and visual impairment (LaGrow & LaGrow, 1983).

In brief, four procedures are used when employing a reversal design:

1. Baseline data are taken for a specific type of response before an intervention is instituted.

2. The intervention is then initiated for a period of time and data are taken on the same type of response.

3. Next, the intervention is withdrawn for a short time to see if the responses go back to the baseline level.

4. If they do, often (though not always) the intervention is reinstituted to see if once again it affects the responses.

Definitions and Distinctions

In addition to the designation *reversal design*, renditions similar to the experimental procedures discussed in this chapter have been described as the *withdrawal design*—because of the temporary withdrawal of the intervention—(Barlow & Hersen, 1984; Tawney & Gast, 1984); the *equiv-*

alent time-samples design (Campbell & Stanley, 1963); the *interrupted time series with multiple replications design* (Cook & Campbell, 1979); and the *within-series elements design* (Barlow, Hayes, & Nelson, 1984). As with other design titles within experimental research, these terms attempt to reflect features of the design's application. Whatever they are called, however, these designs involve the continuous and systematic measurement of some aspect of behavior over time. Which term is used seems to depend on the tradition of research within which a particular author is writing. The designations *reversal* and *withdrawal* stem at least historically from those authors having an orientation toward psychological and clinical work or applied behavior analysis; nomenclatures such as *equivalent time samples* or *interrupted time series* have been used by researchers studying phenomena in naturalistic or applied settings. Multiple designations for this design do appear with regularity in the literature of educational research, and distinctions are made among them in some research texts in which the techniques within each tradition are discussed separately (see the discussion by Huck, Cormier, & Bounds, 1974). Currently, the term *reversal* is commonly used in single-subject experimental research and indicates the attempt in this design to reverse the direction of a response change (Heward, 1987).

Basic Design Characteristics and Guidelines

The reversal design is recognized widely across disciplines as a superior procedure for demonstrating treatment effects. Because it requires the repeated introduction and withdrawal of an intervention strategy, it allows the researcher to make reliable statements about the functional relationship between a set of experimental procedures and related dependent variables (Tawney & Gast, 1984). In their classic book, *Quasi-Experimentation*, Cook and Campbell (1979) indicate that "this design is obviously a very powerful one for inferring causal effects" (p. 222). As such, the reversal design has served as one of the major designs in single-subject experimental research for attributing experimental control to the treatment procedures as opposed to the influence of extraneous variables.

In conventional pretest-posttest control group designs, the demonstration of treatment effects depends on group equivalency through random assignment and a statistically significant difference between experimental- and control-group means on one or more variables. On the other hand, the primary technique of the reversal design for demonstrating treatment effects is the replication or repetition of basic phases within a study and the noting of subsequent changes in the series of responses being measured, as detected by visual inspection of graphs on which the responses have been recorded. The basic phases of the reversal design as might be illustrated when graphing a study's data are seen in Figure 2.1. The repetition of the baseline phase (usually designated as the "A" phase) is shown in (A). In (B), repetition of both the baseline and the intervention condition (the latter usually designated as the "B" phase) is seen.

There are several general guidelines to follow in using reversal designs. Table 2.1 presents a summary of these guidelines, but one that is fundamental relates to whether a researcher should select a reversal design for use in a specific study, rather than choosing another single-subject design. Of primary concern is whether the behaviors under study are likely

Figure 2.1
Graphs Showing the Basic Phases of the Reversal Design

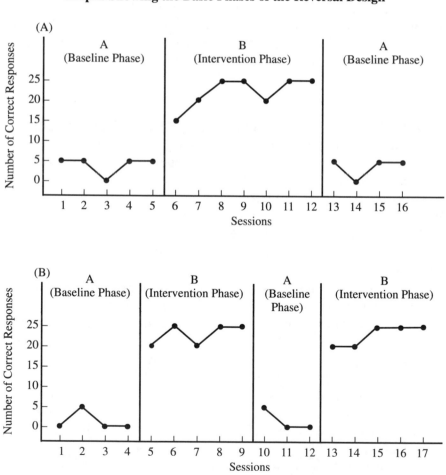

Yaden

Table 2.1
Guidelines for Using Reversal Designs

Internal Validity Considerations

1. Precisely define and carefully delineate the behaviors being measured, the interventions to be implemented, and the procedures to be followed.

2. Collect continuous baseline data until a stable trend is observed.

3. Introduce the intervention or treatment variable only after a stable baseline is achieved.

4. Collect continuous data during the intervention until a stable mode of responding is observed.

5. Only after a stable trend is established during the intervention phase, withdraw the treatment procedures (or, in the case where two contrasting interventions are being examined, after stability has been realized in the first B phase, reintroduce the first intervention).

6. After the second baseline has stabilized, reintroduce the intervention procedures and monitor this condition for at least as long as the preceding baseline. Or, in the case of a study examining two contrasting interventions, after the data for the second A phase intervention is stable, reintroduce the B phase intervention and monitor this phase for at least as long as the preceding A phase intervention.

7. Obtain interobserver, interrater, or interjudge agreement measures to maintain accurate observations of the baseline and intervention responses.

External Validity Considerations

1. Replicate the experiment using the same procedures with new subjects whose characteristics are similar to the original sample. This is called *direct replication*.

2. If appropriate to the question being asked, replicate the experiment with dissimilar subjects, in different settings, or with different researchers, or vary different elements of the experiment. This is called *systematic replication*.

Note: Adapted with the permission of Simon & Schuster from the Macmillan College text *Single-Subject Research In Special Eduaction* by James W. Tawney and David L. Gast. Copyright ©1984 by Macmillan College Publishing Company, Inc.

to return to baseline levels when the intervention is removed. This consideration is necessary because for the reversal design in particular, carryover effects pose special problems in interpreting the influence of a treatment. For example, consider a hypothetical example, illustrated in Figure 2.2. Suppose that a teacher is interested in the impact of familiar selections on a disabled reader's oral reading fluency. In the first baseline or A phase, the student's miscues are recorded for sessions in which there is a reading of each of several unfamiliar passages. During the treatment or B phase, the student is allowed to read the passages and discuss their content with a peer before reading orally to the teacher. During the third or reversal phase, there is a return to the baseline condition, and miscues are again recorded as the student reads unfamiliar passages. Finally, a second treatment or B phase is introduced to attempt to replicate the effects of the intervention that were seen in the first B phase—that is, reduced miscues with familar text.Examination of Figure 2.2 shows that fewer miscues are recorded during the second baseline condition (the reversal phase) than during the first baseline condition, even though the reading of unfamiliar passages was re-instituted during that phase. One likely reason for the student's increased proficiency with unfamiliar passages is that some automaticity in word recognition gained through practice in reading familiar text carried over to the unfamiliar text. Although in this example the presence of carryover effects is a positive sign educationally, if the responses in the reversal phase do not approach the level of those in the original baseline, the reversal design is ineffective for demonstrating the value of a given intervention experimentally. Therefore, in some cases where learned behaviors are the focus of the study, other designs—such as alternating treatments (see Chapter 4 of this volume) or multiple baseline (see Chapter 3)—may be more appropriate.

A second guideline involves the need to establish stable baseline data. Although of somewhat lesser importance with certain other single-subject

Figure 2.2
Graph Showing Data Failing to Return to Original Baseline Levels

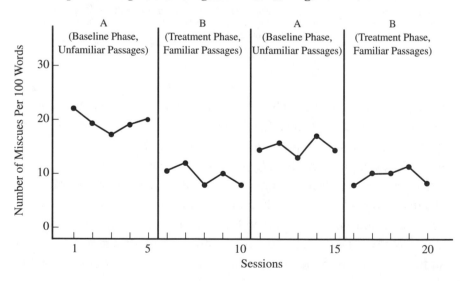

designs (such as in one type of alternating-treatments design described in Chapter 4), baseline stability is crucial in reversal designs for showing the impact of an intervention. As explained in Chapter 1, there are no exact rules about the number of data points needed in a baseline or intervention phase, but the general policy is that there should be at least three to five. However, if baseline data show wide variability from assessment session to assessment session or tend to "drift" (particularly in the direction that would be anticipated as a result of the intervention), then the investigator should wait to introduce the treatment phase until the baseline data stabilize. For example, returning to Figure 2.2, if the intervention had been begun after the third session of the first baseline phase—rather than after the fifth session, as was done—then making a determination about the effect of using familiar text would have been difficult since the baseline miscue measurements during the first three sessions showed a downward trend. If there are phase changes from a baseline to an intervention condition when the behavior is showing an increasing or decreasing trend, then there are problems of interpretation regarding an intervention's effects. More data points during a treatment phase will often help clarify this issue. Causal interpretations from reversal designs depend on the stability of data in the baseline and intervention conditions. If too few data points are gathered to demonstrate this stability, interpretations of treatment effects are extremely limited.

Examples and Variations of the Reversal Design

The examples in the following section represent basic types and variations of the reversal design: a three-phase A-B-A design in which the treatment or intervention is withdrawn and not reinstituted; a standard A-B-A-B format in which one intervention is compared to a no-treatment baseline; an A-B-A-B design in which both the baseline and the intervention phases represent alternative treatments; and an A-B-A-C sequence where in the last phase some additional component is added to the first treatment or another intervention is substituted. These are the main types of reversal designs, but there are several variations in which phases are repeated multiple times, added, combined differently (see Barlow & Hersen, 1984, for an extended discussion), or even integrated with other single-subject design types (cf. Kosiewicz, Hallahan, Lloyd, & Graves, 1982).

The A-B-A Design

The A-B-A design is the simplest example of a reversal format in which conclusions can be made as to the effects of an intervention (Barlow & Hersen, 1984). With this design, the targeted response is specifically delineated and measurement is undertaken repeatedly during each of three phases: (1) a baseline condition, (2) a condition in which the intervention is applied, and (3) a condition in which the intervention is withdrawn (that is, a return to the baseline condition). The logic of this design is that if the desired responses increase over what was seen during baseline and decrease when the intervention is withdrawn, then one can conclude that it is very likely that the intervention was indeed responsible for the improvement.

Suppose, for instance, that a teacher wanted to assess the impact of shared book experiences on a first grade student's word-recognition ability (see Holdaway, 1979; Reutzel, Hollingsworth, & Eldredge, 1994). In the hypothetical example graphed in Figure 2.3, the first baseline phase represents the percentage of target words the child recognized during participation in a reading program where there was regular sustained silent reading intermingled with skill and strategy instruction. During the B phase, the teacher began daily shared book experiences with texts that included the target words and again recorded results from a word-recognition measure. In order to determine whether the student's increased proficiency in the B phase was functionally related to the addition of the shared book experiences to the program, the shared book activity was dropped in a second A or baseline condition. In other words, in this third phase of the experiment

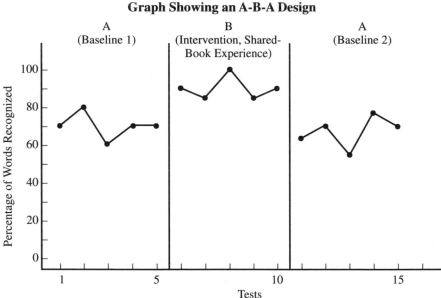

Figure 2.3
Graph Showing an A-B-A Design

the teacher attempted to verify the prediction that the level of word recognition seen during the first baseline phase would continue if shared book experiences were not added.

Given that other threats to internal validity are ruled out (Cook & Campbell, 1979), the A-B-A design allows reasonable inferences about the effects of a treatment. However, one criticism is that the design ends on a baseline phase, therefore denying students the benefit of ending the study with a positive instructional experience. (It should be noted, however, that after seeing the value of an intervention, it is certainly likely in most cases that a teacher would continue the instructional activity after the study proper was terminated.) Although there may be a few cases in which ending on a baseline phase is appropriate—such as in demonstrating the need for a particular kind of intervention (Kratochwill, 1978)—for the most part, adding a second intervention phase is preferable. One of the most important reasons for doing so is the contribution that repeating like phases of an experiment makes to establishing a functional relationship between the independent and dependent variable (see Chapter 1 of this volume). Therefore, A-B-A-B designs, discussed next, which do include a repetition of the treatment condition, have become the benchmark of single-subject experimental studies using reversal designs.

The A-B-A-B Design with One Treatment

One standard four-phase A-B-A-B reversal design involves a no-treatment baseline and a treatment phase, each of which is repeated. Repeating the treatment condition in A-B-A-B designs furnishes two opportunities for confirming the outcomes of the intervention and strengthens the implication that it is indeed the intervention variable, and not uncontrolled factors, that are influencing the responses.

Consider the following hypothetical example. Suppose a researcher wished to examine the effects of using study guides on five sixth graders' responses to questions about chapters they were assigned to read in their science text. Preparing study guides is time-consuming for teachers. Is it worthwhile? Do students show an improvement in their understanding when a study guide directs their attention to important elements in an assigned section? To answer these questions, the researcher might collect baseline data on the total number of correct responses to comprehension questions during a first A (or baseline) phase in which students use no study guide. Then, during the first B phase, the treatment is applied—study guides are used—and data are again collected. During the second A phase, the study guides are withdrawn to determine if student's responses will return to the level where they had been during the first baseline condition.

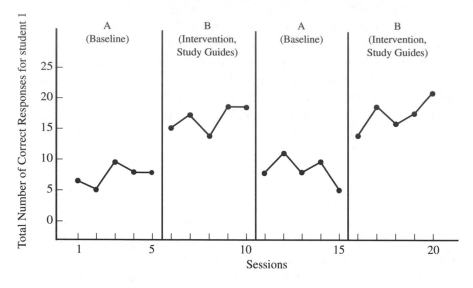

Figure 2.4
Graph Showing an A-B-A-B Design with One Treatment

In the example seen in Figure 2.4 for student 1 in this study, the data in the second A phase do closely approach the level demonstrated in the first A phase. Thus, important information has been obtained for claiming a functional relationship between use of study guides and this student's improved responses. However, by returning to the B phase and having students once again use the study guides, the researcher can gather additional evidence for making this claim. Student 1's data show that a higher level of correct responses is indeed again in evidence during the return to the B phase. Furthermore, the lack of overlap between the data points for the A and B phases provides more assurance that there is a difference between the baseline and treatment conditions. If similar results are obtained for the other four subjects in this study, the researcher will have made a case for the use of study guides with these pupils.

The A-B-A-B Design with Two Treatments

In many situations when literacy studies are conducted, what is generally considered to be the "baseline" in an A-B-A-B design may, in fact, be another set of instructional procedures. In such cases, the A-B-A-B design provides an opportunity for contrasting instructional treatments—for example, a basal reading program versus a literature-based reading program—or perhaps for comparing students' responses to different types of texts.

For instance, several researchers recently have examined the influence of various genres of literature on young children's spontaneous utterances about print during read-aloud sessions (Dahl, 1993; Smolkin, Yaden, Brown, & Hofius, 1992). If such a study were conducted within the tactics of an A-B-A-B design, data patterns illustrated in (A) of Figure 2.5 might be seen. In this hypothetical investigation, during the first A condition, which in this case represents one treatment phase, a child's spontaneous print-related utterances are recorded during several sessions in which picture storybooks are read and discussed during shared book experiences. For the first B phase, the teacher continues the read-alouds and discussions, but this time uses alphabet books, which represents the second treatment. During the second A phase, the reading once again reverts (or "reverses") to the use of storybooks. This is subsequently followed in the second B phase by reverting to the use of alphabet books. As (A) shows, the reversal design can be useful for showing the contrasting effects of treatments—if those treatments can be adequately defined and distinguished.

Another example of use of an A-B-A-B design with two treatments can be seen in the following hypothetical study. In this case a teacher is interested in whether the spelling of a student will improve when instructional attention is directed to a list of self-selected words rather than to words taken from a spelling series. Part (B) of Figure 2.5 represents a series of data points that might result when using a reversal design to study this question. In the first A phase, the results of tests using words from the spelling series are recorded. During the first B phase, test results are based on the student's self-selected list. Although there is an obvious increase in the student's spelling ability during this first B phase, in order to eliminate the possibility of extraneous reasons for the improvement, the self-selected lists are withdrawn and the spelling-series list is reinstituted in the second A condition. The second application of the B condition further verifies the efficacy of using self-selected words to improve this student's spelling ability. The pattern of scores across the A and B treatments was replicated—that is, scores were lower when the spelling-series word lists were used in both A phases and the scores increased both times when the use of the self-selected words was instituted in the B phases—thus, supporting the inference that the use of self-selected word lists did influence the scores.

Both forms of the A-B-A-B design—that is, examining one treatment in contrast to a no-treatment baseline (as described in the previous section) and comparing two interventions (as illustrated in the two examples in the present section)—are considered stronger than an A-B-A design. Although A-B-A designs are still seen, a large number of published studies in the education field today that have employed reversal designs feature those with two A and two B conditions. As pointed out by Tawney and Gast (1984),

Figure 2.5
Graphs Showing Different Examples of an A-B-A-B Design
with Two Treatments

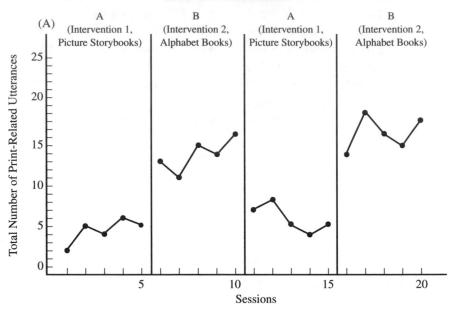

(A)

| A
(Intervention 1,
Picture Storybooks) | B
(Intervention 2,
Alphabet Books) | A
(Intervention 1,
Picture Storybooks) | B
(Intervention 2,
Alphabet Books) |

Total Number of Print-Related Utterances

Sessions

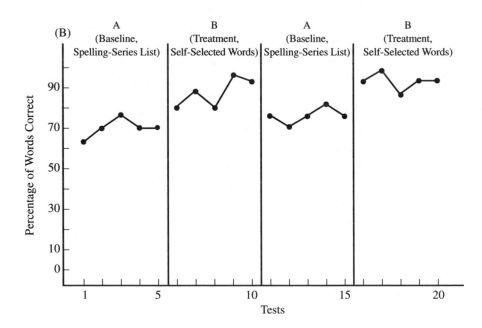

(B)

| A
(Baseline,
Spelling-Series List) | B
(Treatment,
Self-Selected Words) | A
(Baseline,
Spelling-Series List) | B
(Treatment,
Self-Selected Words) |

Percentage of Words Correct

Tests

of all the designs in single-subject experimental research, the "A-B-A-B design permits the most powerful demonstration of experimental control because it requires the repeated introductions and withdrawal of an intervention strategy" (p. 200). Stated in another way, since "replication is the essence of believability" (Baer, Wolf, & Risley, 1968, p. 95), the A-B-A-B design has much to commend it.

The A-B-A-C Design

A hallmark of reversal designs and of single-subject experimental designs in general is their flexibility. Some features of an investigation may be altered after the experiment has started without validity being compromised. This next example illustrates this flexibility.

In the A-B-A-C format, the C condition may represent either an additional treatment or an alteration to the set of procedures originally applied in the B phase. For example, consider the following scenario involving a study designed to determine if teaching story-mapping procedures aids students' recognition of narrative elements and thus improves comprehension. Suppose after seeing the effects in the B phase when story maps were

Figure 2.6
Graph Showing an A-B-A-C Design

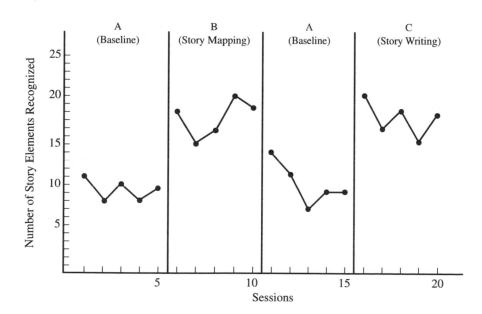

generated after students heard stories read aloud that the researcher decides to add a writing component. So, in the fourth or C phase, rather than generating maps for stories, students are taught to write a story based on a story map supplied by the researcher. In Figure 2.6 a pattern of data for this hypothetical study is illustrated. As the figure indicates, no additional benefit in recognizing narrative elements was seen when children wrote stories based on maps.

A fundamental difference between the A-B-A-C sequence and the standard A-B-A-B format is that in the former there is only one baseline-treatment comparison as opposed to two, since the second and fourth phases are not exactly alike. Though a valid design and one often used in educational research, the A-B-A-C design does not furnish that additional assurance of a functional relationship that is available in the A-B-A-B design. Further verification of results such as those seen in Figure 2.6 would require additional replications of the B and C phases. Such replication is frequently undertaken, resulting in A-B-A-C-A-B-A-C or A-B-A-B-A-C-A or similar designs (see Barlow and Hersen, 1984, for a description of these more complex designs).

Advantages, Limitations, and Considerations of Reversal Designs

As several authorities have noted, the reversal design represents the most fundamental set of procedures in single-subject experimental research for determining the effect of an intervention. Perhaps the most powerful feature of this design is the possibility for at least two replications of the intervention procedure in the same study. As pointed out by Kazdin (1982), the scientific importance of the alternation of the baseline and the intervention phases is that this allows for both the prediction of future responses and a test of that prediction in the same experiment. The repeated A-B alternations give a high degree of certainty that it is the intervention causing the response change and not some other extraneous variable. The multiple replications within the same experiment can also provide some explanations for the internal validity issues of history and maturation, two of the most common threats to time-series experiments (cf. Cook & Campbell, 1979). However, some cautions are in order, as Palincsar and Parecki also mention in Chapter 8.

Perhaps the greatest limitation of reversal approaches is that certain responses, once learned, do not show any deterioration despite removal of the treatment. Of course, when studying cognitive behaviors one usually considers this a positive occurrence. It becomes a problem in reversal designs, however, since the primary strength of the design is the replication of baseline-treatment differences. Baselines that do not return to or at least approach their original levels render inferences about the impact of treatments difficult to make.

Another limitation is that staff involved in an investigation are sometimes unwilling to remove a treatment that benefits the subjects involved (Barlow & Hersen, 1984). For healthcare researchers and those dealing with certain special education populations, for example, this is a definite problem. Particularly in cases where a child is involved in self-injurious behavior, an intervention that prevents further danger to the child should not be removed. This presents less of a problem in most literacy studies, however, especially since withdrawal to baseline phases occurs for only a very limited time. Further, Sulzer-Azaroff and Mayer (1977) have suggested that it is not always requisite for responses to reverse entirely to the baseline level of performance. It is often sufficient for demonstrating experimental control if several sessions of measurement show a level of from one-third to two-thirds of the level seen during the intervention phase.

Removal of a treatment may also cause "resentful demoralization" (Cook & Campbell, 1979). Although Cook and Campbell conceptualize this threat to internal validity as pertaining to a control group not receiving a beneficial treatment, demoralization may apply to a subject or subjects who, once having the benefit of the intervention, resent that it is being withdrawn. Thus, their responses are influenced by angry or depressed attitudes that have an additional effect during the return-to-baseline period.

Summary and Conclusions

This chapter presented some basic elements of single-subject reversal designs and provided examples of this approach based on topics of interest within the literacy community. The research examples discussed here show possible applications of reversal approaches to literacy studies and offer suggestions as to how such investigations could be undertaken within a single-subject experimental research framework.

Reversal designs with removed treatments and multiple replications can be applied to any number of situations. However, it is not the design per se that brings "elegance" or insight to a research situation, it is rather the creativity and knowledge of the investigator coupled with the sensitive application of the tools of inquiry. It is my hope that this chapter has enabled other literacy researchers to gain insight into how to use this single-subject design to further our knowledge about literacy growth.

References

Baer, D.M., Wolf, M.M., & Risley, T.R. (1968). Some current dimensions of applied behavior analysis. *Journal of Applied Behavior Analysis, 1,* 91–97.

Barlow, D.H., Hayes, S.C., & Nelson, R.O. (1984). *The scientist practitioner: Research and accountability in clinical and educational settings.* New York: Pergamon.

Barlow, D.H., & Hersen, M. (1984). *Single case experimental designs: Strategies for studying behavior change* (2nd ed.). New York: Pergamon.

Bullis, M., & Anderson, G. (1986). Single-subject research methodology: An underutilized tool in the field of deafness. *American Annals of the Deaf, 131,* 344–348.

Campbell, D.T., & Stanley, J.C. (1963). *Experimental and quasi-experimental designs for research.* Chicago, IL: Rand-McNally.

Cook, T.D., & Campbell, D.T. (1979). *Quasi-experimentation: Design and analysis issues for field settings.* Chicago, IL: Rand-McNally.

Dahl, K.L. (1993). Children's spontaneous utterances during early reading and writing instruction in whole language classrooms. *Journal of Reading Behavior, 25,* 279–294.

Heward, W.L. (1987). Reversal and alternating treatments designs. In J.O. Cooper, T.E. Heron, & W.L. Heward (Eds.), *Applied behavior analysis* (pp. 163–194). Columbus, OH: Merrill.

Holdaway, D. (1979). *The foundations of literacy.* Sydney, Australia: Ashton Scholastic.

Huck, S.W., Cormier, W.H., & Bounds, W.G. (1974). *Reading statistics and research.* New York: HarperCollins.

Kazdin, A.E. (1982). *Single-case research designs: Methods for clinical and applied settings.* New York: Oxford University Press.

Kosiewicz, M.M., Hallahan, D.P., Lloyd. J., & Graves, A.W. (1982). Effects of self-instruction and self-correction procedures on handwriting performance. *Learning Disability Quarterly, 5,* 71-78.

Kratochwill, T.R. (1978). *Single subject research: Strategies for evaluating change.* New York: Academic.

LaGrow, S.J., & LaGrow, J.E. (1983). Consistent methodological errors observed in single-case studies: Suggested guidelines. *Journal of Visual Impairment and Blindness, 77,* 481–488.

Luetke-Stahlman, B. (1986). Gaining methodological insight through use of single-subject designs in hearing-impaired classrooms. *American Annals of the Deaf, 131,* 349–355.

McReynolds, L.V. & Thompson, C.K. (1986). Flexibility of single-subject experimental designs. Part I: Review of the basics of single-subject designs. *Journal of Speech and Hearing Disorders, 51,* 194–203.

Reutzel, D.R., Hollingsworth, P.M., & Eldredge, J.L. (1994). Oral reading instruction: The impact on student reading development. *Reading Research Quarterly, 29,* 40–65.

Siegel, G.M., & Young, M.A. (1987). Group designs in clinical research. *Journal of Speech and Hearing Disorders, 52,* 194-199.

Smolkin, L.B., Yaden, D.B., Brown, L., & Hofius, B. (1992). The effects of genre, visual design choices, and discourse structure on preschoolers' responses to picture storybooks during parent-child read-alouds. In C. Kinzer & D. Leu (Eds.), *Literacy research, theory and practice: Views from many perspectives* (41st yearbook of the National Reading Conference, pp. 291–302). Chicago, IL: National Reading Conference.

Sulzer-Azaroff, B., & Mayer, G.R. (1977). *Applying behavior-analysis procedures with children and youth.* New York: Holt, Rinehart & Winston.

Tawney, J.W., & Gast, D.L. (1984). *Single-subject research in special education.* Columbus, OH: Merrill.

CHAPTER 3

Multiple-Baseline Designs

James Kucera
Saul Axelrod

Individuals engaging in literacy research often want to determine which interventions will result in reading improvements. The researcher, whether a teacher, university professor, or program coordinator, strives to determine if a particular intervention is responsible for positive changes in students' reading responses, attempting to isolate any functional or causal factors in improved reading behaviors. Research approaches that can be used to analyze questions of academic performance include correlational studies, experimental–control-group research, qualitative studies, and single-subject experimental investigations. The researcher must determine the most appropriate methodology to address the question under study by eliminating those less suitable while matching desirable features of designs to the question or questions.

One type of single-subject research design that is particularly well suited to literacy research is discussed in this chapter. We explain the logic and basic characteristics of the multiple-baseline design and describe three subtypes of it—that is, multiple-baseline designs (1) across behaviors, (2) across individuals, and (3) across settings. Properly undertaken, the multiple-baseline design can help researchers discover effective methods for reading instruction.

Logic of the Multiple-Baseline Design

In Chapter 2, Yaden describes the logic and characteristics of the reversal design. With that design the researcher first measures the baseline (preintervention) rate or level of a response—such as the frequency of disruptive behavior during reading. Next, the experimental variable (intervention) is introduced. The intervention in this example might consist of mailing complimentary letters to parents when a child's disruptive behavior decreases. In the return-to-baseline phase, the teacher might stop sending the letters. If the frequency of disruptions increases to baseline rates following the reversal to baseline conditions, then we can make a credible case that sending the letters had a functional relationship with the improvement in behavior.

Despite its demonstrated usefulness with a variety of problems, the reversal design's utility is less clear in investigations of certain academic skills and strategies. In some cases, after students have experienced effective instruction the behavior being studied will not return to baseline levels when the intervention is removed. In those instances, the effectiveness of the instruction can neither be supported nor refuted using a reversal design. In contrast, the multiple-baseline design may be useful in cases where the skill or strategy being taught (the dependent variable) is not reversible. The multiple-baseline design does not require a return of the academic response to baseline levels to demonstrate functional and cause-and-effect relationships (Baer, Wolf, & Risley, 1968). Thus, this design is well suited for some types of research in which reading behaviors, once learned, may not reverse. The multiple-baseline design is also appropriate for conditions in which it is not desirable for a behavior to reverse (Baer, Wolf, & Risley, 1968; Barlow & Hersen, 1984). This feature is particularly appealing to literacy researchers when it seems undesirable to tolerate even a brief, temporary decline in a student's academic responses to demonstrate the effectiveness of a procedure.

The multiple-baseline design involves taking repeated measures of preintervention (baseline) performance concurrently on two or more dependent variables. (Although a minimum of only two dependent variables is necessary, it is more convincing to use three or more.) Once the baseline rate for each dependent variable is stable or the trend is predictable (see Chapter 1, this volume), the researcher introduces the independent variable (such as an instructional method), applying it only to the first dependent variable, and continues to repeatedly measure the reader's performance on all the dependent variables. This means that data are collected on those dependent variables still in the baseline condition at the same time that data are collected for the dependent variable experiencing the intervention. Figure 3.1 gives an example. The first tier in Howard's graph shows that in week 2, instruction begins on set 1 of the letters targeted for identification. But the second and third tiers of his graph indicate that sets 2 and 3, using different targeted letters, are still in the baseline condition during week 2. Although sets 2 and 3 have not yet been the focus of the in-

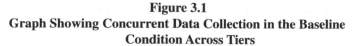

Figure 3.1
Graph Showing Concurrent Data Collection in the Baseline Condition Across Tiers

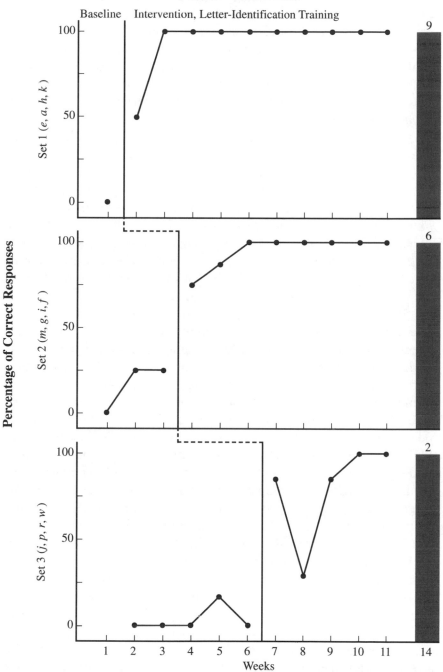

Note: Adapted from Wedel, J.W., & Fowler, S.A. " 'Read me a story, Mom': A home-tutoring program to teach prereading skills to language-delayed children," *Behavior Modification*, 8, 245–266. Copyright 1984 by Sage Publications, Inc. Reprinted by permission of Sage Publications, Inc.

tervention, data continue to be taken for his responses to those two sets during this time.

If the reader responds favorably to the intervention's application to the first dependent variable, the researcher introduces the procedure to the second one (in Howard's case, the second set of letters); if the procedure results in a favorable response with the second dependent variable, it is introduced to the third, and so forth. The researcher continues to take baseline measurements on any reading strategies and knowledge targeted as dependent variables that are not yet receiving the intervention. All data are graphed, and the researcher determines the effectiveness of an intervention by looking at the graphs. A functional relationship is indicated if the student's performance changes only in response to the intervention.

Staggering the initiation of the independent variable with each of the dependent variables is a critical component in this design. It allows the researcher to infer a verification of the prediction that the baseline behaviors would have remained at their demonstrated level if the intervention had not been applied (see Chapter 1). If all the intervention phases were started at the same time, then some coincidental factor could be responsible for observed changes. However, it is unlikely that some other factor would coincide with the beginning of *all* the intervention phases.

In a properly controlled design as many confounding variables as possible are eliminated (Campbell & Stanley, 1963). (See Palincsar and Parecki, Chapter 8, this volume, for examples.) High levels of internal validity—the degree to which the independent variable alone is responsible for the changes in the dependent variable—are a critical goal of experimental research. One potential threat to internal validity is history, defined as specific events occurring during the intervention phase—in addition to the independent variable—that might affect the dependent variable. Unplanned events extraneous to the experiment that might affect a child's performance, such as changes in a classroom reading program or a change in teachers, are examples of this type of confounding effect. The staggered start of the intervention phases in the multiple-baseline design is key to demonstrating control over this threat to internal validity.

There are certain constraints in using this design, however. For example, inherent to the multiple-baseline design is the assumption that a method that affects one specific type of reading response will (1) affect a similar type of response; (2) affect the same reading response in different settings; or (3) have the same effect on the type of response in another student (Risley, 1969). If the researcher does not have reason to believe that the independent variable will have an effect on each dependent measure of interest in a study, then the multiple-baseline design is inappropriate for the question being asked.

Kucera & Axelrod

Another constraint on selection of dependent variables is that they must be functionally independent of one another—that is, they cannot co-vary. For example, let us say that an independent variable, play training, is introduced and changes in frequency of fantasy play (the dependent variable) are recorded. At the same time, however, the other responses still in baseline (frequency of mastery play and group play) also change. In this example, someone might ask, "Is an extraneous variable at work (thus the change in the dependent variable cannot be attributed to the independent variable of play training), or are all these responses related to one another and likely to be affected by the change in the first response?" Similarly, if the dependent measures involved the comprehension of three similar stories, for example, then improvement following initiation of an intervention in the first condition with the first story could reasonably generalize to the other stories while they were still in the baseline phase. Although a teacher may be pleased to see improvement in all the target areas at the cost of only one intervention, experimental control has been lost. In this case, changes in the dependent variable could not be directly attributed to the independent variable. Thus, researchers need to select dependent variables carefully when using a multiple-baseline design.

Given these constraints, however, the multiple baseline can be used with different behaviors for the same student, the same behavior for different students, or the same behavior for the same student in different settings. Characteristics of these versions of multiple-baseline designs are discussed in the next sections, and general tips on using them appear in Table 3.1.

Table 3.1
Tip Sheet for Using Multiple-Baseline Designs

1. Clearly define both the dependent and independent variables prior to the study in terms that are observable, countable, testable, and measurable. Generally target three or more dependent variables.

2. Begin all baselines at the same time. Apply the intervention only when baseline data indicate a stable level and trend.

3. Apply the intervention to the next dependent variable when it is evident that a positive response has been attained from the intervention on the preceding dependent variable.

4. Have someone conduct reliability checks for both the dependent and independent variables (see McCormick, Chapter 1, this volume).

5. Collect and graph data daily, using a separate tier for each dependent variable.

Multiple-Baseline-Across-Behaviors Design

In this variation of the multiple-baseline design, the investigator collects baseline measurements of several different responses (such as editing writing for capitals, commas, and spelling) for a period of time for an individual child. Once a stable baseline is well established for all responses, an intervention (such as peer conferencing) is applied to one behavior (use of capital letters) while baseline conditions remain in effect for the others. Continuous assessments of all three behaviors are conducted. If changes in this first behavior are attained, then the intervention is applied to the second behavior (commas). Following replication of these effects with the second behavior, the intervention is applied to the third behavior (spelling), and so on. Consequently, if each response improves when the intervention is applied, we can be reasonably assured that there is a functional relationship between the intervention and these responses.

Wedel and Fowler (1984), for example, used this design to assess the effectiveness of a home-tutoring program that involved parents in teaching letter- and word-knowledge skills to their language-delayed children. Study subjects were four mother-child dyads, one of which was Howard and his mother (see Figure 3.1). The intervention focus for Howard was on letter knowledge, which the teacher assessed weekly. During the baseline weeks of the program, Howard's mother read and discussed storybooks with him without providing any letter-knowledge training. After a baseline period, the teacher asked Howard's mother to focus on teaching him four letters (*e*, *a*, *h*, and *k*). Specifically, the intervention consisted of the mother stopping at the end of each page of the story, targeting one letter for instruction by saying the letter, and then asking the child to identify it. As indicated in Figure 3.1, the transition from the baseline to the intervention phase between weeks 1 and 2 for the first set of letters shows a steep ascending slope of the line in set 1 following the beginning of home tutoring (the independent variable). Data recorded to the right of the vertical condition or phase line indicates an immediate and powerful response to the intervention.

Baseline data collection for sets 2 and 3 was continued during the intervention for set 1 letters for the first two weeks. Then, while continuing the instruction on set 1 letters, Howard's mother began the intervention during week 4 for the second set of letters (*m*, *g*, *i*, *f*). This was begun after the positive effect in set 1 could be seen. Once again, after intervention began for the second set, the graph showed an improvement in letter identification. Continuing the instruction with set 1 and set 2 letters, in week 7 Howard's mother initiated the intervention for the third set of letters (*j*, *p*, *r*, *w*). As shown in the graph, although acquisition of letter identification was slowest for set 3, the intervention improved Howard's knowledge of these letters as well. This is also evident from posttests (maintenance scores) given at the end of formal training 9, 6, and 2 weeks later, of which all indicated 100 percent recall.

This study clearly demonstrated the positive impact of this type of home tutoring for helping Howard develop letter knowledge. The power of this conclusion is based on the abrupt and continuing improvements in letter identification following application of the independent variable. The staggered start of the interventions demonstrates the results of the intervention in all three sets by replicating the effect only when the intervention is introduced.

For another example, we will examine a hypothetical study on writing instruction using this design. Samantha, a fourth grader, had difficulty writing stories, as evidenced by a lack of story elements in her narratives. The teacher-researcher was interested in assessing the potential impact of a strategy designed to encourage Samantha to monitor her uses of these story elements in her writing by graphing the number of these elements each time she wrote a story. This self-monitoring strategy constituted the independent variable. The dependent variables consisted of a scale for assessing the schematic structure of stories by means of six story grammar elements (adapted from Graham & Harris, 1989) arbitrarily assigned in pairs as follows: (1) main character and locale; (2) goal and reaction; and (3) time of story and ending. For each element, a score of 0 was assigned if the element was not present, and a score of 1 was assigned if the element was included. Highly developed elements could each receive a score of 2. Consequently, scores could range from 0 to 4 for each dependent variable, with a total possible story grammar score of 12 (calculated by adding response scores together).

Prior to the intervention, baseline data were collected on the number of story elements contained in Samantha's short stories. As shown in Figure 3.2, the baseline data were collected simultaneously on all dependent variables. Starting in session 5, Samantha was taught to graph the number of instances of her use of main character and locale elements in her stories. As indicated in the figure, Samantha increased her use of the main character and locale elements from an average of 1.5 to 2.7 following this intervention. Meanwhile, the other baselines remained stable, indicating a lack of covariance between the dependent variables.

After some improvements in the first dependent variable were observed, beginning in session 9, Samantha was taught to graph the second dependent variable (goal and reaction). Then, following a favorable trend in the second dependent variable, the experimental variable was applied to the final condition (time of story and ending) in addition to the first two. Samantha's use of elements related to time of story and ending elements

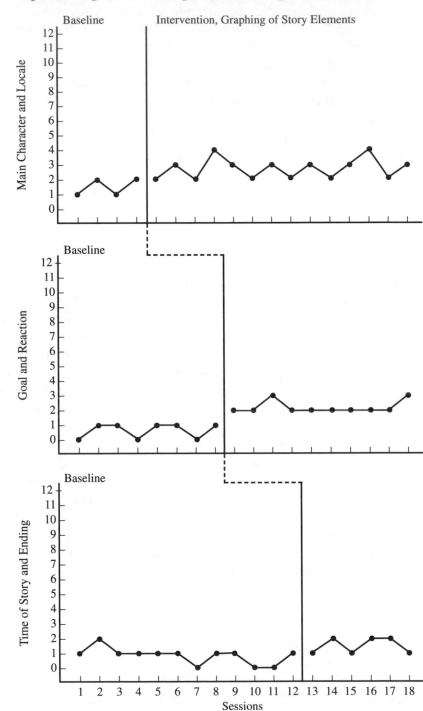

Figure 3.2
Graph Showing Use of a Multiple-Baseline Design Across Behaviors

Kucera & Axelrod

increased in some sessions following initiation of self-monitoring, but not in others.

The multiple-baseline-across-behaviors design demonstrated that the independent variable of self-monitoring by graphing used in this hypothetical study was responsible for some modest improvements in Samantha's use of story grammar elements in writing. The research design supports this conclusion since, in general, the improvements in Samantha's writing occurred only following each intervention, and similar improvements did not occur in the absence of intervention. However, there is considerable overlap in the data points between the baseline and intervention conditions, especially in conditions 1 and 3. Thus, the results of this example indicate that although the self-monitoring provided by graphing helped somewhat to increase the use of story elements, it did not appear to be particularly powerful. It is likely in this case, then, that the teacher-researcher would want to examine other avenues for helping Samantha improve her writing.

Bianco and McCormick (1989) used a slight variation on this design to assess the effectiveness of a curriculum for teaching students outlining as a study skill. The subjects were high school students with learning disabilities, and the program included three categories (or independent variables) to be learned. The categories were title or main topic selection and format, subtopic selection and format, and detail selection and format. Students read and outlined material daily. The dependent variable was each student's performance as measured on a checklist of content selection and outlining skills.

As can be seen in Figure 3.3, at no point did the students demonstrate outlining skills during their baselines. Program instruction first began with the category of title or main topic selection and format. The students' response to the program of instruction was immediate and favorable, climbing to four of four elements correct on the task analysis. Meanwhile, baseline data continued to be collected in the two other categories. Next, the researchers initiated the program in the subtopics category, and subsequently with details. The students' outlining skills improved noticeably in each category following instruction.

You will recall that in the study with Howard and his mother (Wedel & Fowler, 1984), maintenance was measured by posttests administered several weeks following the intervention. In the present case, the researchers also continued to collect dependent measures following cessation of the intervention, but did so during the study proper (see Figure 3.3). The data collected during this postinstruction phase indicated the durability of the outlining skills after the instruction had been terminated. However, since these data represented a measure of short-term maintenance, follow-up checks were also conducted after four weeks and eight weeks, with the

Figure 3.3
Graph Showing Multiple-Baseline Design Across Behaviors, with Maintenance Measures

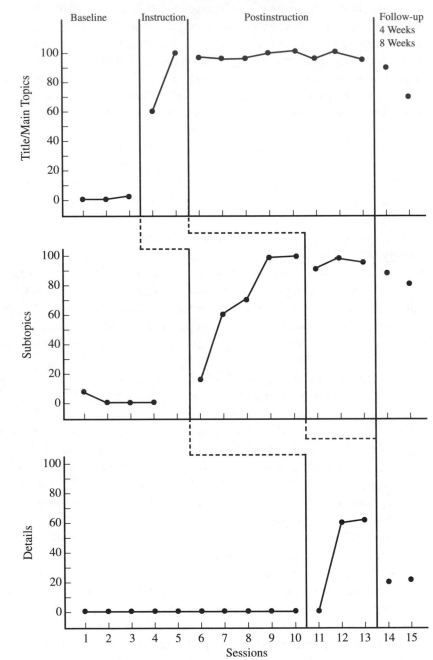

Note: Adapted from Bianco & McCormick (1989). *Journal of Educational Research, 82* (5), 286. With permission of the Helen Dwight Reid Educational Foundation. Published by Heldref Publications, 1319 18th St., NW, Washington, DC 20036-1802.

level of response in the first two categories faring better than that of the third. As can be seen, the postinstructional and follow-up phases followed the same multiple-baseline format as the preceding phases and were plotted on the same graphs. (This study also provides an example of one in which transfer measures were undertaken; for details see Bianco and McCormick, 1989.)

As shown in these examples, the multiple-baseline-across-behaviors design is well suited for addressing many literacy questions. One caveat, however, should be considered prior to initiating a study with this design: as mentioned above, dependent variables need to be carefully selected to ensure that they are functionally independent of one another (so that baselines of still untreated behaviors remain unaffected) and yet are similar enough for each to respond to the same intervention.

Multiple-Baseline-Across-Subjects Design

Whereas the studies discussed in the preceding section examined different behaviors for the same subjects, the across-subjects design addresses the impact of the independent variable on the same behavior (or response) for different subjects. After a stable baseline on a particular response or behavior is established with each student, the independent variable (intervention) is applied to one student while maintaining baseline conditions for the others. When some evidence of improvement is noted in the first subject's response, the independent variable is then provided to both the first and the second student. If the response of the second student improves, then the intervention is provided to the next student, and so on until all the students in the study have been exposed to the intervention. The logic of the design, then, is based on the premise that if each individual improves when the intervention is applied to him or her, it is likely that the intervention caused or is functionally related to the improvement in behavior.

Shapiro and McCurdy (1989) used the multiple-baseline across-subjects design to determine if a specific type of modeling strategy (using a taped-words format) could foster improvement in word recognition. (Although they examined contextual reading and comprehension as well, we will discuss only the part of their study in which they compared the effects of two approaches to increasing word-recognition proficiency.) The two conditions consisted of (1) practice in simply reading a list of words (in this case, taken from a driver education manual), and (2) practice that incorporated modeling through the use of an audiotape. Subjects were ninth and tenth graders with behavior disorders who were reading at or below the sixth grade level.

As shown in Figure 3.4, during the baseline phase, each of the five subjects was asked to read aloud a list of vocabulary words. Each list was read twice, and the number of words read per minute correctly and incorrectly (the dependent variable) was recorded for the second reading. Figure 3.4 indicates that subject 1, for example, read an average of 28 words per minute correctly in baseline (across the four sessions) and 8 words incorrectly. Following the fourth session, showing a decline in the rate of words read correctly during baseline by subject 1, the intervention began for this subject while the other four subjects continued in the baseline condition. As illustrated in Figure 3.4, following the intervention in the fifth session, subject 1 read 30 words per minute correctly and 10 words per minute incorrectly.

For the intervention (the independent variable), the student was asked to read along with an audiotape of the same words, recorded at 80 words per minute. After the initial reading, the student was asked to read the list again, and the investigator recorded words read correctly and incorrectly. As indicated in Figure 3.4, the intervention phase showed an improvement in the number of words read correctly by the student. Then, as noted by the vertical dashed line running between the tiers of the graph, the intervention began for subject 2 while the other three students remained in baseline. Once subject 2 showed some improvement, the intervention phase was subsequently applied to the next subject, as indicated by the dashed condition line. The same pattern can be seen for four of five subjects: an increasing trend for words read correctly between baseline and intervention phases, and little difference between baseline and intervention for the number of words read incorrectly.

Overall, the results of this study demonstrate a modest effect of the taped-words method versus gains seen from practice alone. If the taped-words intervention had been more effective, the intervention phase of the graph would have had a steeper slope than the baseline for the number of words read correctly. Instead, changes in the slope between the baseline and intervention phases are relatively small, indicating that the taped-words intervention showed only a slight improvement over practice alone.

As this example illustrates, by staggering the introduction of an intervention across individuals, the multiple-baseline design can be used to analyze the potential benefits of an intervention for different individuals. This type of design enables teachers to answer questions concerning how to differentiate instruction for groups of students, allowing them to provide the most powerful intervention for individuals. However, it should be noted that although staggering the intervention is a strength, it can also be a liability in some circumstances. Prolonged baselines for students in need of intervention may not always be educationally sound.

Figure 3.4
Graph Showing Multiple-Baseline Design Across Subjects

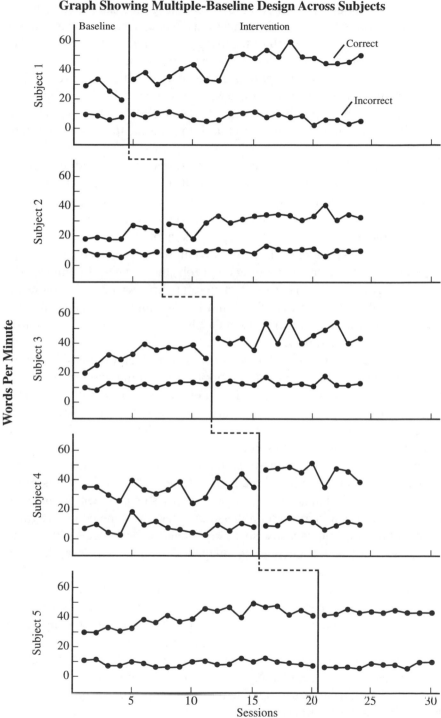

Multiple-Baseline Across-Settings Design

This variation in the multiple-baseline design measures one behavior (dependent variable) of an individual but in different settings. After baseline measurements are taken in all of the settings, the intervention is applied to the behavior in only one setting. If the behavior improves in the first setting or situation, then it is applied in the second setting, and so on. The logic of this design is based on the assumption that if the dependent measure shows improvement in each setting when and only when the independent variable is applied, then a functional relationship has been demonstrated.

Imagine, for example, that a teacher-researcher wanted to increase children's voluntary reading in his class during free time each day. The teacher was particularly interested in Amy, since Amy was the one pupil who almost never selected reading as her activity choice. Because of her resistance, the teacher enlisted Amy's parents in an effort to foster more independent reading. Baseline data consisted of the teacher and the parents independently observing and plotting on graphs the number of minutes Amy read per day over a five-day period when left to her own devices. Figure 3.5 shows baseline data for the school and for the home, demonstrating exceedingly few minutes on any given day in either setting that Amy chose to pick up a book and read.

As the graph in Figure 3.5 indicates in typical multiple-baseline fashion, intervention was begun in the school setting while baseline data continued to be collected in the home. The intervention consisted of three parts: (1) the teacher expressed to the children his wish that they would choose to read during some of the free-time period; (2) the teacher showed two trade books per day and told something interesting about each; and (3) the teacher said that he was going to read during this time and that he would sit with the children while he read—and then he did so. After this intervention was instituted at school on day 6, Amy's engagement in independent reading began to increase in that setting, as can be noted on the graph by the number of minutes now spent in this endeavor. However, the graph also shows that she was not reading independently at home, where the baseline condition was still in effect.

Since there was a stable and increasing trend in the school-setting data, on day 10 her parents began the same intervention used in the classroom at home. Each day, Amy's mother or father expressed the desire for her to spend some time reading her books, they talked about two books from her home library, and then one parent sat with Amy, reading his or her own book while she read. Again, as demonstrated by the data points in Figure 3.5 for the home setting, when this intervention was initiated there was an increase in the time Amy read independently. Two things attest to the

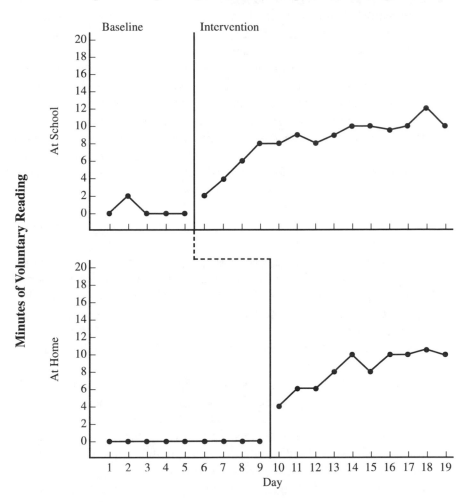

Figure 3.5
Graph Showing Multiple-Baseline Design Across Settings

strength of the intervention: (1) there was no increase at home without the intervention, while there was an increase at school with the intervention; and (2) the intervention initiated at home showed the same positive trend as seen when initiated at school.

As this hypothetical example illustrates, the multiple-baseline design used across settings may address an issue of generality important to literacy researchers. However, the researcher must scrutinize carefully the integrity of the independent variable (see Chapter 1 of this volume), since it is possible that different individuals will carry out the intervention in the different settings.

Advantages and Limitations of the Multiple-Baseline Design

Probably the most important advantage of the multiple-baseline design is that with it, the researcher can determine the effectiveness of an instructional strategy without withdrawing the intervention, as is required by the reversal design. This is especially helpful when a return to baseline conditions is not likely or desirable. This feature is particularly important in literacy research for analyzing such independent variables as cognitive strategies, which, once they are learned, may not be reversed to baseline levels. In addition, multiple-baseline designs allow researchers to examine changes in multiple responses. For example, as we saw in the discussion of the across-behaviors design, a number of behaviors can be subject to intervention in one study. In this respect, multiple-baseline designs can be an efficient technique for analyzing more than one dependent variable.

Another advantage exists in the across-subjects design. In this design, gathering information on several students' responses to an intervention can help the researcher assess the effects of an instructional approach and note individual variation in response to the intervention (Axelrod, 1983). It can also provide replications of the experiment across subjects that may attest to the reliability of the results. Further, some degree of generalizability can be attained by replicating the design with different subjects, enabling researchers to a build a better theoretical understanding of an intervention.

The flexibility of multiple-baseline designs allows researchers to adjust to a variety of circumstances. For example, a researcher can address problems of apparently confounding variables by extending the baseline until it is stable. Finally, these designs are relatively easy to conceptualize and provide researchers with useful tools for evaluating the effects of an intervention for a wide range of skills and responses.

Multiple-baseline designs, however, are not problem-free. Perhaps their most serious limitation is the necessity of selecting dependent variables that are independent of one another. If they are not, then a change in one may bring about a change in the other, thus making it impossible to evaluate the effects of the independent variable. At the same time, however, these variables must share enough similarity that each can be changed through a single intervention. In essence, the dependent variables must be functionally similar, but cannot covary.

In addition, the multiple-baseline design is not appropriate to use when the dependent variable must be changed quickly. For some behaviors to stabilize, for example, prolonged baselines will be necessary, but even a moderate wait during the initial baseline period may be too costly for the student who is not being helped. Ethical issues are raised when researchers have to postpone interventions. Furthermore, in some cases, researchers may have difficulty taking regular measurements over extended periods.

In conclusion, literacy researchers can use the multiple-baseline design as a powerful tool in certain circumstances for defining the factors that will make students better learners. In the examples cited in this chapter, university faculty, teachers, and parents effectively carried out these investigations in classrooms and in their own homes. Consequently, the results of the research can provide direct assistance to both the investigators as teachers and the subjects as learners.

References

Axelrod, S. (1983). *Behavior modification for the classroom teacher* (2nd ed.). New York: McGraw-Hill.

Baer, D.M., Wolf, M.M., & Risley, T.R. (1968). Some current dimensions of applied behavior analysis. *Journal of Applied Behavior Analysis, 1*, 91–97.

Barlow, D.H., & Hersen, M. (1984). *Single case experimental designs* (2nd ed.) New York: Pergamon.

Bianco, L., & McCormick, S. (1989). Analysis of effects of a reading study skill program for high school learning-disabled students. *Journal of Educational Research, 82*(5), 282–288.

Campbell, D.T., & Stanley, J.C. (1963). *Experimental and quasi-experimental designs for research*. Chicago, IL: Rand-McNally.

Graham, S., & Harris, K.R. (1989). A components analysis of cognitive strategy instruction: Effects on learning disabled students' compositions and self-efficacy. *Journal of Educational Psychology, 81*, 353–361.

Risley, T.R. (1969, April). *Behavior modification: An experimental-therapeutic endeavor*. Paper presented at the Banff International Conference on Behavior Modification, Banff, Alberta, Canada.

Shapiro, E.S., & McCurdy, B.L. (1989). Effects of a taped-words treatment on reading proficiency. *Exceptional Children, 55*, 321–325.

Wedel, J.W., & Fowler, S.A. (1984). "Read me a story, Mom": A home-tutoring program to teach prereading skills to language-delayed children. *Behavior Modification, 8*, 245–266.

CHAPTER 4

Alternating-Treatments Designs

Susan B. Neuman

In literacy research what is the most effective way to evaluate how alternative approaches affect student performance? Because this question is so important, it is raised frequently. One basic purpose of conducting literacy research is to find out how effective various instructional strategies or approaches are, either for one individual student or for a group. In such investigations, researchers often select a methodology that compares a treatment group with a control group, using inferential statistics to determine the relative effects of the intervention. However, in many cases, the sample size, as well as the variability within the group (some subjects change and some do not), may provide insufficient evidence for concluding that one method is better than another.

The alternating-treatments design provides an alternative approach for examining the relative effects of two or more interventions. It is both an experimentally sound and an efficient method to measure the performance of a particular student (or groups of students) on a target behavior. In this form of single-subject research, two or more distinct treatments are introduced, usually following a brief baseline phase. The treatments are then alternated randomly and continued until one treatment proves to be more effective than the others, or until it is clear than no method is superior to another. During the entire experiment, the learner's performance for each treatment is plotted on a graph, and the effects of the treatments can be discerned easily by visual analysis. These procedures control for many possible threats to the internal validity of a study, such as differential selection of subjects or history effects.

Figure 4.1 provides an example of this design. Suppose a researcher was interested in examining the impact on students' comprehension performance of a technique called *previewing* (a detailed form of written ad-

Figure 4.1
Graphs Showing the Alternating-Treatments Design with Three Learners and Three Treatments

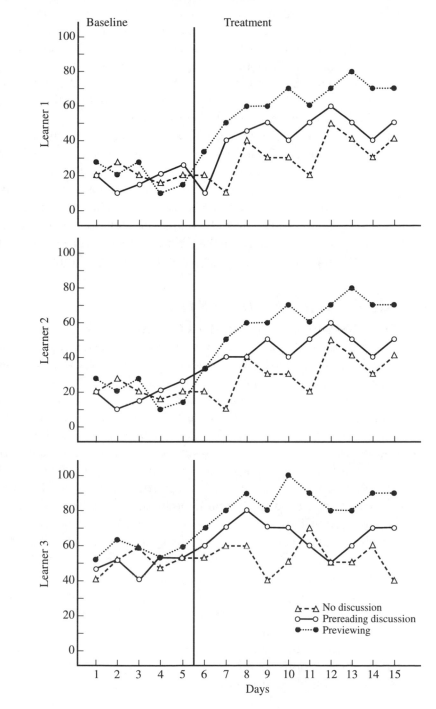

vanced organizer developed by Graves, Cooke, and LaBerge, 1983) compared to a prereading discussion or a no-discussion control condition. In this hypothetical example, assume that after each treatment, students read a passage and then were administered a 10-item comprehension measure. The order of the treatments was counterbalanced over a 10-day period, with each treatment applied in random order each day. In other words, each intervention had to "take turns" in terms of when it was applied. As noted in Figure 4.1, the data for each of the three learners, plotted separately for each intervention, clearly indicate that the previewing strategy in this case was more effective than the other treatment or control condition.

The alternating-treatments design has several important advantages for research and instruction. It can be used to compare different approaches relatively quickly, allowing for instructional decision making. The graphs are easy to interpret since the data points for each treatment are displayed simultaneously. Further, this design can be used to examine applied questions within the context of instruction, with minimal interference to ongoing classroom activity. These advantages make the alternating-treatments design extremely useful for investigators of language and literacy learning.

Basic Characteristics of the Alternating-Treatments Design

Various names have been used to refer to this design, such as *multielement design* (Sidman, 1960), *simultaneous treatment design* (Kazdin & Hartmann, 1978), and *multiple schedule design* (Hersen & Barlow, 1976). To reflect the emphasis on experimental manipulation, however, Barlow and Hayes (1979), Cooper, Heron, and Heward (1987), and Houlihan, Jones, Sloane, and Cook (1992) have recommended calling it the *alternating-treatments design*, the designation used in this book. The fundamental characteristic of this design is the alternating of two or more distinct treatments (independent variables) while observing the result on a particular behavior (dependent variable). Other characteristics of this design are summarized in Table 4.1.

Unlike many other single-subject designs, the alternating-treatments design does not require that baseline data be collected over a period of time. However, a baseline condition is always desirable and is used in several variations of the design described later in the chapter. Whether a baseline is used or not, in an alternating-treatments design, the student may experience different interventions from session to session, or different interventions at different times on the same day. In both situations, the order in which the interventions are presented is randomly counterbalanced to increase the possibility that effects are due to experimental rather than to extraneous conditions. For example, Figure 4.1 illustrates a hypothetical study focusing on the impact on comprehension of previewing (PV) and prereading discussion (P) versus a no-instruction or baseline (B) condition. In such a study, the order of treatments might appear as follows:

Sessions

1	2	3	4	5	6	7	8	9	10
P	P	B	B	B	PV	PV	P	P	PV
B	B	PV	P	P	P	P	B	PV	P
PV	PV	P	PV	PV	B	B	PV	B	B

In this example, all three conditions were administered at different times in one day. In session 1, for example, students engaged in a prereading discussion prior to reading a short story. Then they were given no prior

Table 4.1
Summary of the Alternating-Treatments Design

Basic feature	Alternating two or more treatments
Time factor	Treatments can be alternated within sessions, across time of day, on different days; counterbalancing required
Baseline condition	Not required; if used, does not have to be stable Baseline can be continued throughout experiment as a condition if comparisons are desired.
Standard variations	Alternating treatments with no initial baseline Alternating treatments with initial baseline Alternating treatments with initial baseline and final treatment phase
Internal validity	Demonstrated when patterns of response vary with the alternating condition and there is minimal overlap among conditions If one intervention is consistently associated with a higher level of responding, internal validity is good, indicating good experimental control
External validity	Effects must be replicated across sample, different samples, different behaviors, and/or different conditions
Major advantages	Baseline not required Speed of comparison high Sequence effects minimal
Major considerations	Susceptible to multiple-treatment interference and carry-over effects Treatments must differ significantly from one another Not effective for assessing the impact of an independent variable that produces change slowly or needs to be consistently administered over a continuous period of time

treatment, followed by a different story. Finally, in the reading period scheduled later in the day, students received a preview followed by a third story. Comprehension assessments were administered at each time. Subsequent sessions on following days were designed to counterbalance when and in what order the treatments were administered.

Note that there are several important considerations in using this design. First, it is predicated on the principle that the two or more treatments are distinct. In this case, previewing is clearly different from a prereading discussion or no treatment at all. To determine their distinctiveness, it might be helpful to imagine whether an observer who knew nothing about the study could readily discriminate among the different treatments. If not, students can not be expected to respond differently to the supposedly different procedures.

Second, it is important that the treatments being compared are able to show behavioral change session by session (or blocks of sessions, if that is the unit of analysis) (Barlow & Hayes, 1979). For example, if it typically takes numerous successive sessions for a strategy treatment to affect an outcome, such as the frequency of higher order verbalizations, it would not be wise to use an alternating-treatments design. This is because the treatments do not occur on consecutive sessions but are ordered randomly.

Third, like the other designs described in this book, the alternating-treatments design is based on frequent and direct measurement of the target behavior. In traditional large-group experimental designs, judgments about the relative effectiveness of a treatment or treatments are usually determined by comparing pre- and posttest assessments. However, in the case of the alternating-treatments design, the researcher measures the behavior of interest continuously. Thus, in the earlier example a comprehension measure is given following each treatment, allowing the researcher to follow the course of the experiment as it is being conducted. Similarly, it is important to measure the target behavior directly in its context. In the earlier example, comprehension assessment was based on the actual short story just read, not on a standardized reading achievement test.

How does the researcher determine whether one treatment is more effective than another? In traditional experimental research, the issue of significance has often been interpreted mathematically by determining whether the differences in the dependent variable are statistically significant. In single-subject experimental research, the question of whether such differences are significant is an educational one. Through visual inspection of graphs displaying levels of student response, the data paths are used to examine the degree of experimental control. This refers to objective, believable evidence that the introduction of the treatment is accompanied by a change in the trend and level of the target behavior (Kratochwill, 1978).

When the paths of two or more treatments show no overlap with one another and the trend of each path is replicated with each introduction of the same treatment, then a clear demonstration of experimental control is indicated (Cooper, Heron, & Heward, 1987). Such is the case in Figure 4.1 where there are minimal overlaps, indicating a clear picture of differential effects.

Of course, not all analyses provide such a clear picture. More often than not, there will be some overlap between treatments. In fact, many graphs cannot be interpreted unambiguously. In the example shown in Figure 4.2, notice the degree of overlap for all three conditions in the beginning of the experimental period. In this hypothetical study, two interventions are introduced to promote word recognition. While scores for the two treatments begin to separate from the baseline after several sessions, these two conditions overlap for the remainder of the investigation, demonstrating little difference between the two interventions. Calculating average percent of the number of words recalled accurately across each condition verifies that neither condition is superior to the other, but that both are more effective than no treatment. The degree of difference is discerned by looking at the distance between the two treatments and the baseline.

As was noted earlier, experimental control was clearly demonstrated between the previewing treatment and the discussion and no-treatment conditions shown in Figure 4.1. The vertical distance between the data paths

Figure 4.2
Graph Showing Overlap Between Treatments

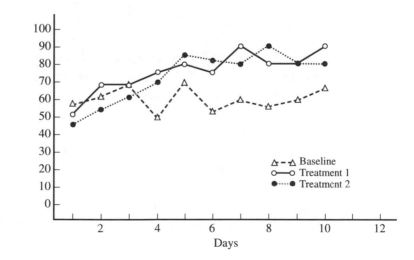

consistently revealed higher comprehension scores for those in the pre-viewing treatment than in the other two conditions. Now, it is important to ask the next question: Does the average 20 percent differential significant-ly contribute to a student's comprehension of written text? Many educa-tors would agree that this magnitude of increase, particularly for poor read-ers, represents an educationally significant effect.

The alternating-treatments design is usually considered high in inter-nal validity because of continuous measurement and the degree of experi-mental control. The counterbalancing of treatments also reduces sequencing problems because no one treatment is consistently introduced first and maintained for an extended period. If these procedures are followed, then one can say with reasonable assurance that the results of the experiment are due to the treatment, and not to other confounding variables. Internal va-lidity, therefore, is demonstrated when the patterns of response (compre-hension scores as in Figure 4.1) vary with a particular condition, with min-imal overlap between conditions. Consequently if one intervention is consistently associated with higher levels of responding, then one can as-sume that the internal validity is good.

The issue of generalization, however, is a bit more tricky. Tradition-ally, experimental studies using statistical significance imply generaliz-ability and replicability to other samples within a similar population (though replications may not be done). In the case of the alternating-treatments design, however, external validity or generalizability is said to be demonstrated only when the differential effects of the intervention are ac-tually replicated by other subjects within the same population, across dif-ferent populations, or across different behaviors (see Chapter 1 of this vol-ume). A later part of this chapter explains how a number of researchers have attempted to resolve this issue.

Types of Alternating-Treatments Designs

In this section, three types of alternating-treatments designs are de-scribed and illustrated. They are (1) alternating treatments with no initial baseline, (2) baseline followed by alternating treatments, and (3) baseline followed by alternating treatments with a final treatment phase. These three major variations of alternating-treatments designs are the ones most com-monly found in the literature. Although these designs are used in special ed-ucation and other fields of research, each is relatively new to investiga-tions in language and literacy. Check Appendix C for additional examples of literacy studies that have used the alternating-treatments design (or some variation).

No Initial Baseline

Unlike most designs in single-subject experimental research, a baseline condition is not always necessary with an alternating-treatments design. Rather, the investigation may actually be initiated by simply alternating the selected interventions. This may be especially useful when baseline data are difficult to obtain, or when it might not be appropriate to deny treatment, even for a brief phase.

Although a baseline is not necessary, it may be included as one of the treatments to be compared in the investigation. The term *baseline* refers here to a no-treatment condition. For example, perhaps a teacher is interested in determining whether a visualization technique might enhance a child's ability to recognize words. In the treatment condition, the teacher might prompt the child to use the technique, whereas in the baseline, or no-treatment condition, the teacher would simply encourage the child to guess. Although one could argue that encouragement to guess is itself a strategy, it could be defined as a baseline treatment if it represented a strategy commonly used by the teacher prior to the study.

In using this design, Tawney and Gast (1984) suggest that the investigator should do the following:

1. Operationally define the independent and dependent variables.
2. Determine a schedule for counterbalancing the presentation of the treatments across time.
3. Introduce the interventions in an alternating fashion.
4. Continue until there is enough evidence to suggest the effectiveness (or lack of effectiveness) of one intervention over the others.

This type of alternating-treatments design can be used creatively to examine a host of interesting educational questions. For example, Figure 4.3 shows a two-treatment alternating-treatments design. In this case, the question is, "Does the correction of significant miscues in oral reading affect a student's fluency in reading?" In treatment 1, the child's significant miscues are corrected, and a fluency measure follows; in treatment 2, significant and insignificant miscues are corrected, and a similar measure follows. Notice that different treatments are given on different days. For example, on day 1, the teacher institutes treatment 1; on day 2, also treatment 1; on day 3, treatment 2; and so forth. Also, notice that in this study a second replication could be conducted in another classroom, perhaps with special needs students, to examine the degree of replicability and generalizability across settings.

The versatility of this type of alternating-treatments design is evident in that it can examine not only different interventions or different teachers

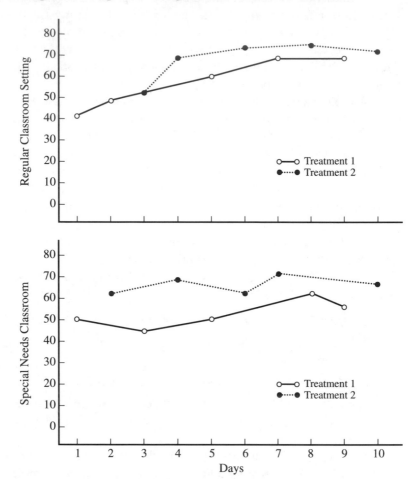

Figure 4.3
Graphs Showing Alternating Treatments with No Baseline

but behavior in different contexts. Neuman and Daly (1993) devised a study of this type to analyze differences in teenage mothers' interactions with children in the context of three different activities: reading, sociodramatic playing, and instructing. Each mother was trained in scaffolding techniques designed to build "bridges of understanding" between the teenagers and their children. Then, mothers and children were involved in all three activities daily for 15 minutes, with the order of activities randomly counterbalanced each day. For example, on day 1, a mother first read a story to the children, then played, and then provided an instructional activity, such as putting together a puzzle. On the next day, this order was rearranged so that it began with play. Figure 4.4 shows the percent of scaffolding utterances for one mother across each of the 3 activities for 12 sessions. Although no differential effects were observed in the first few sessions, from about session 5 on it is clear that maternal utterances for "bridge building" were far more evident during play than during storybook reading and instruction. But note that these data do not provide evidence of the effects of training on mothers' scaffolding behavior. To do this, the study would have required a preintervention baseline level of behavior. This points to a limitation in what inferences can be drawn from this particular variation of the alternating-treatments design.

Regarding external validity, there can be little support for making inferences, on the basis of one case, that the independent variable (here the play context) fills an influential role in maternal scaffolding exchanges. Even if one could isolate the actual variables in this context through a rigorous, step-by-step analysis, it would still be difficult to argue for any kind of generality. To build a case requires replication. In this study, the experiment was replicated four additional times, with four different participants in a similar setting. As Figure 4.5 indicates, in four of the five cases, the percentage of utterances was higher in the play context than the others, arguing for a degree of generality. However, we cannot assume broad generalizability even at this level. To build an even stronger theoretical case, further studies would be needed to examine these effects in a different setting with

Figure 4.4
Graph Showing an Alternating-Treatments Design Across Contexts

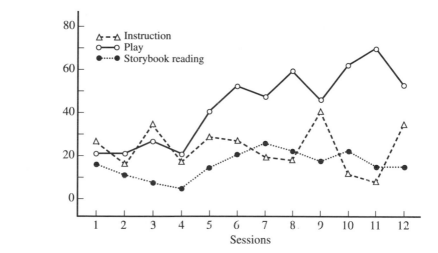

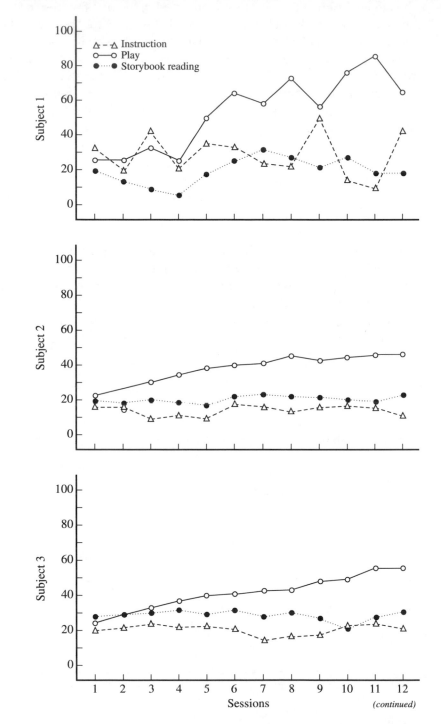

Figure 4.5
Graphs Showing Replication of an Alternating-Treatments Design

Neuman

Figure 4.5
Graphs Showing Replication of an Alternating-Treatments Design (cont'd.)

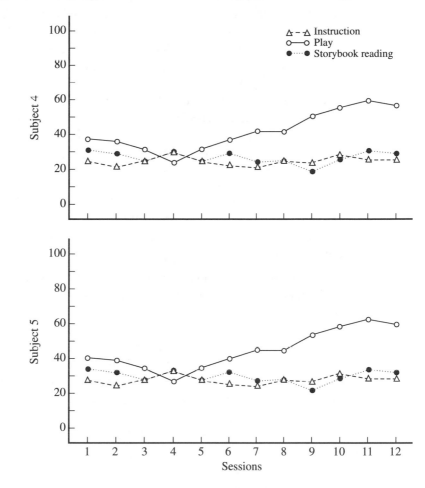

different individuals. As with most good research methods, this single-subject design requires continuing replication across settings and among different participants.

Use of an Initial Baseline

Ideally, it is best in most situations to collect baseline data on the target behavior before beginning the intervention. Unlike other single-subject designs such as reversal or multiple baseline, however, this variant of the alternating-treatments design does not require that the baseline be stable.

Rather, the baseline period may simply represent several consecutive sessions of data collection that give the researcher evidence about the target behavior prior to intervention. For example, a researcher might collect fluency rates on selected stories for three to five sessions before introducing two alternating treatments designed to enhance oral reading fluency.

The researcher also has the option of continuing the baseline (or no-treatment) condition during the course of the study. This allows him or her to observe not only the differential effects of two or more treatments, but the relative effectiveness of treatment versus no treatment at all. Such an analysis may provide a strong case for some types of intervention.

When using this type of alternating-treatments design, the investigator should do the following:

1. Follow points 1 and 2 specified by Tawney and Gast (1984) for the alternating-treatments design with no baseline (see page 71).

2. Collect baseline data on the target behavior (dependent variable) for a number of sessions.

3. Introduce the interventions in accordance with the counterbalancing schedule (and, if desired, continue to collect baseline data throughout the study).

A study by Rose and Beattie (1986) provides an example of an alternating-treatments design incorporating an initial baseline, two alternating treatments, and a continuing baseline condition. Their study examined the relative effectiveness of two approaches for enhancing oral reading accuracy. During the first five days, students individually read a short story aloud without any advance preparation while the teacher recorded all miscues. The number of words read correctly by each student was calculated. The alternating-treatments phase of the study that followed this baseline involved three different conditions of approximately three to four minutes, presented in random order on separate days. In condition 1, *listen*, the teacher read an assigned passage orally while the student followed along. In condition 2, *tape*, the student was instructed to turn on the tape recorder and follow along as the passage was read aloud. Following conditions 2 and 3, the student read a short story aloud, and miscues were recorded. Baseline, or no treatment, constituted condition 3, which was continued throughout the study.

As illustrated in Figure 4.6, data points in the first five sessions reflect the baseline condition. These graphs indicate that both the *listen* and the *tape* conditions resulted in more words read correctly per minute than the baseline condition. Experimental control, although not complete because of slight overlapping of the data paths for student 4, is also demonstrated be-

Figure 4.6
Graphs Showing an Alternating-Treatments Design with a Continuing Baseline Condition

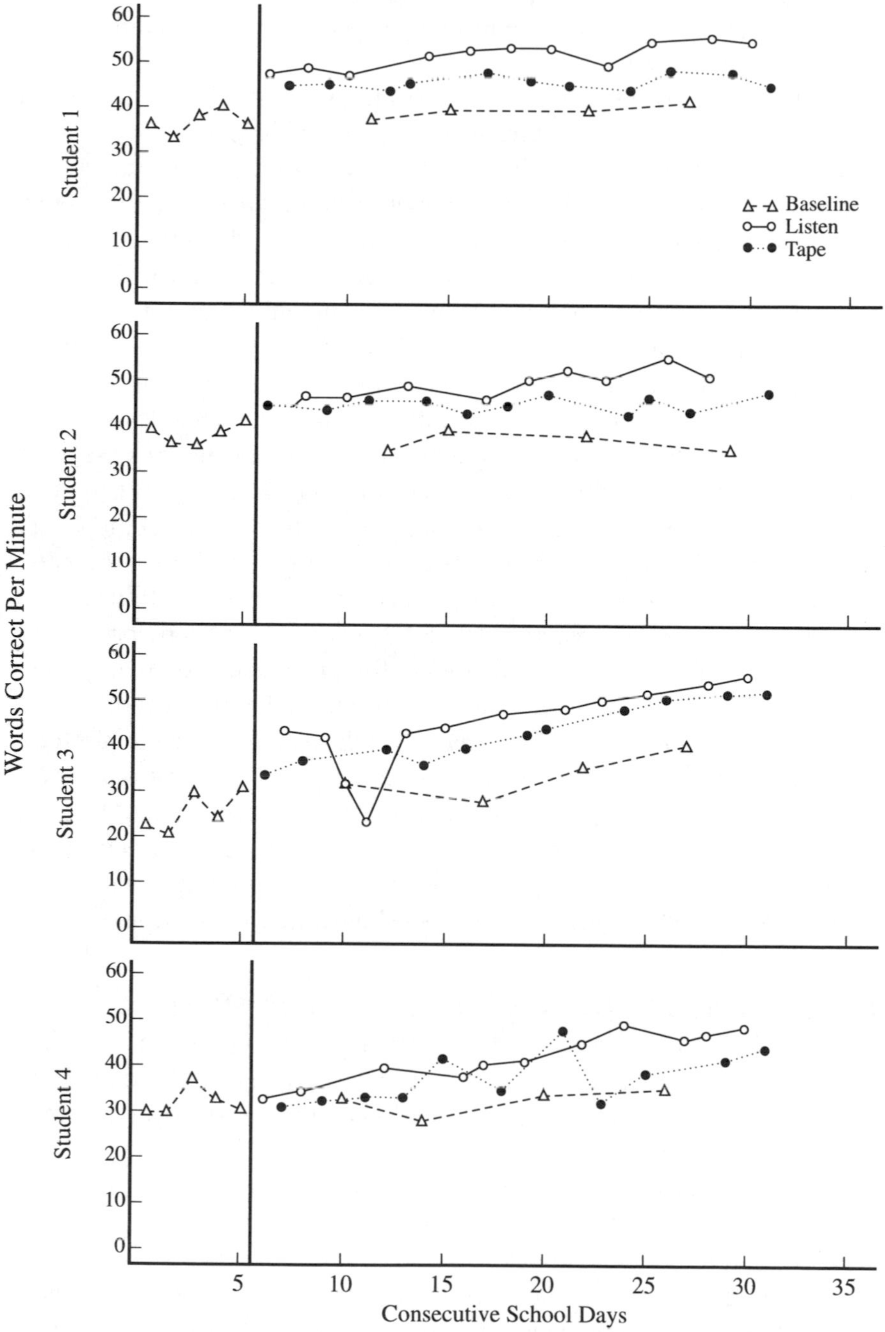

Note: From "Relative Effects of Teacher-Directed and Taped Previewing on Oral Reading," by T.L. Rose and J.R. Beattie, *Learning Disability Quarterly, 9*, p. 196, 1986. Copyright 1986; reprinted by permission of the Council for Learning Disabilities.

tween the listening intervention and the tape intervention. These data for each learner, with the exception of student 4, show that the listening procedure was related to higher performance levels than was the taped presentation. Even for student 4 the listening procedure was generally related to greater oral reading accuracy.

There are several important features in this study. First, the use of a no-treatment control as one of the alternating variables provides a valuable indicator of the impact of the alternating interventions, demonstrating these effects even more powerfully than a preintervention baseline period alone. Second, this study illustrates an important advantage of single-subject design: it is clear simply from looking at the graph that the vertical distance between treatments and control is smaller for student 4 than for the others. Thus, this analysis allows us to look at differential effects among students, a crucially important phenomenon often overlooked in group studies.

Literacy researchers new to the alternating-treatments design might ask how these data are best reported in research studies. In this case, Rose and Beattie (1986) describe their results by displaying the graphs and by reporting in their text on median performance levels for baseline, tape, and listening procedures. Since the differences in the graphs are not dramatic, the authors report that the "listening intervention was found to be related to relatively higher performance levels.... However, [the tape procedure] may be the preferred approach if teacher time is considered an important variable..." (p. 198). Thus, in contrast to traditional experimental studies that use the term *statistical significance* to indicate a benchmark of effects, terms providing more explanatory information—such as *somewhat better*, *superior to*, or *slightly higher performance*— are preferred in this design. In addition, the researchers in this study carefully delimit their findings to the sample population. In fact, they make special recommendations that the study be replicated by other researchers using similar populations.

Initial Baseline with a Final Treatment Phase

An alternating-treatments design using an initial baseline and a final treatment phase is the most widely used design variation for examining the effects of different treatments on special populations (Cooper, Heron, & Heward, 1987). The variation consists of three phases: an initial baseline phase, a middle phase comparing two or more treatments, and a final phase in which only the most effective treatment is provided (Cooper, Heron, & Heward, 1987). The design has several advantages. First, it provides the researcher with strong evidence that the impact of a particular treatment is not due to a multiple-treatment effect (that is, the combined effect of treatments). Second, if the effects are sustained, it provides some indication that they are not due to the immediacy of the intervention but may continue past the experimental period.

When using this variation, the investigator should do the following:

1. Operationally define the independent and dependent variables.
2. Determine a schedule for counterbalancing the presentation of the treatments across time.
3. In the second phase of the design, introduce the interventions in an alternating fashion, according to the established counterbalancing schedule. (Baseline may be continued for comparison with interventions.)
4. Continue with the most effective intervention (based on the second phase) in the final phase of the study. Baseline observations are no longer conducted.

The following hypothetical case provides an example of this variation of alternating treatments. Assume that a collaboration between a teacher and a researcher from a local university led the two professionals to be interested in comparing the effects of two different approaches to "grand conversations" in the classroom. The objective was to encourage more interpretive comments and questions among the students than normally occurred. For the study, the teacher divided the classroom into three heterogeneous groups, termed "interpretive communities." During the initial baseline period, data were collected on the number of interpretive idea units produced by students in each group for 10 minutes daily over a period of 5 days, without any teacher intervention (see Figure 4.7). Then, following baseline, grand conversations were held twice weekly for a 30-minute period. Each group was exposed to three different conditions for 10 minutes each during each session. In condition 1, *baseline*, the teacher did not become involved in the group at all, but encouraged students to interact on their own. In condition 2, *start-up*, the teacher began discussion on a particular topic in the grand conversation, but then stepped back and became an observer. In condition 3, *participant*, the teacher acted as a conversational partner along with other members of the group. Conditions were counterbalanced for all three groups. The researcher collected data throughout the study by observing and audiotaping each group. The alternating treatments were maintained over a 16-week period, during which the teacher and researcher examined the graphed data on an ongoing basis. It became apparent that students engaged in more interpretive interactions when the teacher became a partner in the grand conversation (condition 3). Thus, in the final phase of the study, the three groups received only this condition.

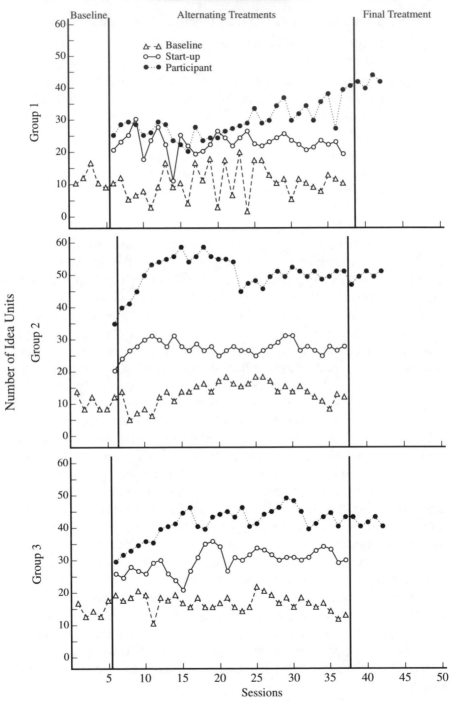

Figure 4.7
Graphs Showing an Alternating Treatments Design with Baseline and Final Treatment Phases

Neuman

This variation of the alternating treatments design provides the teacher and researcher with valuable data that enable students to receive the most effective treatment in the final phase for the entire instructional period. This example also illustrates how the alternating-treatments design can be used appropriately when the unit of analysis is a group of students, rather than an individual. This unit of analysis is appropriate here because the question of interest involved the collective performance of the group in "interpretive conversation" and not an individual response.

Considerations in Using Alternating-Treatments Designs

Despite positive features of the various alternating-treatments designs, some basic considerations may make the design inappropriate for particular research questions. As always, it must be the research question that drives the methodology, and not the other way around.

One key problem with this design is *multiple-treatment interference.* This term refers to the confounding of effects due to the presence of other treatments and the possibility that the effects of one treatment may be influenced by or carry over to another treatment. What is evidenced, therefore, is actually due to a combination of treatments rather than one treatment alone. This is a serious issue because *multiple-treatment interference* can make it impossible to attribute the effects of a target behavior to a particular treatment. This can be particularly troublesome to literacy researchers and may limit the kinds of questions that can be answered by the alternating-treatments design. Consider, for example, the case of contrasting the effects on comprehension of a guided visualization strategy with a verbal think-aloud approach during reading. Even with counterbalancing treatments, it may be obvious to the researcher after several sessions that the guided visualization strategy is being used to organize how the individual thinks aloud. In this case, one treatment may influence how the other treatment is used.

These concerns mean that the researcher who uses the alternating-treatments design must select independent variables carefully to avoid contaminating one treatment with another. This may be difficult in studies in which behaviors are specifically transferable to other behaviors. However, in the hands of a researcher knowledgeable about cognitive processes and how they can be reflected, the use of alternating-treatments design is an attractive option. There are many examples of interesting topics that may be addressed using this design, such as the following:

• effects of oral versus silent reading on comprehension

- impact on inferencing ability of an analogical reasoning strategy versus a structured overview or no treatment
- relative effects of prediscussion, postdiscussion, or no discussion on student interpretations of text.

Therefore, although researchers must clearly be sensitive to multiple-treatment interaction and carryover effects, the kinds of questions they can address with alternating-treatments designs are potentially exciting.

A second concern is that the very nature of the alternating-treatments design limits the types of treatments that can be analyzed using this methodology. The treatments must have important variations—the design is not effective for examining subtle distinctions between treatments. For example, it would not be appropriate to examine differences between two treatments both involving some form of drill—such as two forms of worksheets—since it is likely that children would not be aware of the differences between the two. Rather, the treatments must be quite distinguishable, like the differences between direct instruction versus inductive teaching.

Third, the treatments themselves must be potentially powerful enough to demonstrate reasonably immediate effects. For example, it would not be wise to examine the effects of sustained silent reading versus strategic instruction on the percent of time spent reading, because it may take multiple sessions before the investigator might observe real changes in the dependent variable on the basis of the treatment.

Finally, treatments that are developed over a consecutive series of sessions cannot be measured using the alternating-treatments design. For example, if it typically takes a three-step procedure over a three-day period for a phonics program to improve a student's reading performance, this procedure would not be an appropriate choice to study using this design, since the design relies on the counterbalancing of treatments. In choosing alternating treatments, then, the investigator must select procedures that can reasonably be alternated within classroom instruction. For example, consider a study of prediscussion versus postdiscussion or no discussion on the number of interpretive idea units that a particular group engages in while reading social studies texts. In this case, the treatments are easily distinguishable, the effects can be discerned reasonably efficiently, and the alternation should not be overly disruptive or confusing to the students.

Thus, although the alternating-treatments design is an elegant and efficient method for comparing the effects of different treatments, some constraints need to be considered when employing this design in language and literacy research. Being aware of these constraints, and organizing treatments and procedures accordingly, will enable investigators to use the design to their advantage in answering critical questions in educational research.

The alternating-treatments design is a practical and efficient technique for examining the effects of two or more treatments. It can be especially useful in cases where baseline data are not available or are highly variable. Comparisons between treatments can be made rather quickly, and the technique is highly applicable for educational decision-making in naturalistic contexts. Several important considerations, however, may influence a researcher's use of the alternating treatment design. As always, the investigator should be careful to weigh these advantages and considerations in the light of the research questions being raised. If used wisely, however, the alternating-treatments design could prove to be a new, highly valuable method for examining critical questions in language and literacy research.

References

Barlow, D.H., & Hayes, S.C. (1979). Alternating-treatments design: One strategy for comparing the effects of two treatments in a single subject. *Journal of Applied Behavior Analysis, 12*, 199–210.

Cooper, J.O., Heron, T.E., & Heward, W.L. (1987). *Applied behavior analysis*. Columbus, OH: Merrill.

Graves, M., Cooke, C., & LaBerge, M. (1983). Effects of previewing difficult short stories on low ability junior high school students' comprehension, recall, and attitudes. *Reading Research Quarterly, 18*, 262–276.

Hersen, M., & Barlow, D.H. (1976). *Single case experimental designs: Strategies for studying behavior change*. New York: Pergamon.

Houlihan, D.D., Jones, R.N., Sloane, H.N., & Cook, J. (1992). Brief report: An extension of the sequential alternating treatment design using reversals with subjects not available concurrently. *Behavioral Residential Treatment, 7*, 71–77.

Kazdin, A.E., & Hartmann, D.P. (1978). The simultaneous-treatment design. *Behavior Therapy, 5*, 912–923.

Kratochwill, T.R. (1978). *Single-subject research: Strategies for evaluating change*. New York: Academic.

Neuman, S.B., & Daly, P. (1993, December). *Guiding young children: A family literacy approach*. Paper presented at the National Reading Conference, Charleston, SC.

Rose, T.L., & Beattie, J.R. (1986). Relative effects of teacher-directed and taped previewing on oral reading. *Learning Disability Quarterly, 9*, 193–199.

Sidman, M. (1960). *Tactics of scientific research*. New York: Basic.

Tawney, J.W., & Gast, D.L. (1984). *Single-subject research in special education*. New York: Macmillan.

CHAPTER 5

Statistical Analysis Procedures for Single-Subject Designs

Michael L. Kamil

Decisions about experimental outcomes have been made by single-subject researchers primarily through visual analysis of graphed data (see Chapters 1–4 of this volume). Early developers of this methodology devised and progressively refined designs through which conclusions could be drawn by examining changes in level and trend of responses as exhibited through data points graphed during all phases of a study. However, as early as 1974, journals focusing on single-subject investigations began publishing articles advocating use of statistical analyses as a supplement to visual inspection of data in certain circumstances (see, for instance, several articles in the *Journal of Applied Behavior Analysis*, volume 7). Kazdin (1976), an early proponent of the single-subject experimental paradigm, suggested that statistical comparisons are useful as an adjunct to visual analysis in five circumstances—when (1) visual examination does not provide a convincing demonstration of results in one direction or another; (2) elusive effects might be identified that conceivably could be overlooked with visual inspection alone; (3) the researcher has not been able to establish a stable baseline in those designs where a stable baseline is demanded; (4) a moderate improvement in responses is seen during the baseline condition, and statistical treatment might reveal an educationally significant accelerated trend during intervention; and (5) external events may have periodically skewed data during less-controlled observations in real-life settings. Other researchers combine visual and statistical tests to strengthen the illustration of effects for potential consumers (see, for example, Mudre & McCormick, 1989; Palincsar & Brown, 1984).

Linking graphic appraisal and statistical procedures in single-subject experimental research remains controversial in some quarters, but a growing number of investigators take the tack proposed throughout this volume—that is, they coalesce methods of exploration and evaluation when this enhances their capability to answer the research question at hand. This chapter provides further rationale, as well as guidelines, for the statistical analysis of data in research with an *n* of one or with a small group where data for individuals are examined.

The Use of Statistics in Single-Subject Designs

Statistical procedures are used to determine to what degree measurements of phenomena vary. That is, if we measure more than one occurrence of the same event, the results will usually be different if the measurement is sufficiently sensitive. The use of statistics allows researchers to determine whether those differences in measurement are chance occurrences or the result of some systematic characteristic in the population. Put another way, statistics tell us how sure we can be that any differences we have measured are real. "Real" differences, in this case, are those that will occur often if the same measurements are performed repeatedly. If the differences are not "real," they are due to chance variation or some other artifact.

The fact that we know before we begin an investigation that individuals differ from one another on many dimensions causes a problem for educational (and other) research. We would be surprised if everything (or anything!) we measure about an individual was the same for every other person. One way to solve this is to use large numbers of individuals so that the quantity of measurements will tend to even out any unusual or chance differences. Another way to solve this problem is implicit in the topic of this volume—to restrict measurements to a single individual. In these cases, we assume that most of the background variables are the same from measurement session to measurement session and the only variables that should change dramatically are those that we are manipulating in the research. However, once we choose this attractive alternative, we are faced with two other problems: we must question the reliability of our measurements and we must make a choice of whether to perform statistical analysis on the data we collect and, if so, which procedures to use.

The problem of reliability is particularly acute. Researchers often make the unwarranted assumption that the variables in their research are highly reliable. This assumption is typically *not* made when tests and other instruments are involved. In these cases, it is normal to measure how reliable the measures are. More important is the notion that all measurement is subject to error. It is difficult to dispute this tenet, so it must be addressed directly. Simply put, reliability involves the concept that a single measure is always in error. For highly reliable measurements (variables, instruments, etc.) the error will be small; for less reliable measurements, it will be greater. When we are dealing with the behavior of a single individual, the reliability of the instrument assumes a greater importance, since chance differences may not "even out" over a larger number of cases.

The second problem is that many statistical tests are based on the principle of large numbers. That is, statistical analyses often depend on the use of a large number of cases or observations to make inferences about the differences among any observed differences.

In the discussion that follows, I will attempt to show some alternative solutions to these problems. In each case, it is important to understand several cautions. First, there is almost never a single answer to the question "Which statistical procedure should be used in this situation?" Rather, each statistical procedure has advantages and disadvantages and several alternatives may have equally attractive qualities. Second, the choices of statistical procedures are limited by the research design and methodology. For example, the use of a single individual with single measurements over time will require a different statistical procedure from a case in which a number of individuals are studied over time and their results aggregated for later analysis. Finally, as in other research, it is more efficient to use statistical analyses to answer questions that are generated by theoretical concerns before the study is conducted rather than after the data are collected.

It is critical to understand that the design of a study determines what sorts of statistics are appropriate. It is not possible to guarantee that every data set can be analyzed statistically in a meaningful way. If a single-subject design has too few observations, it may be impossible to establish a probability level that will ensure confidence in the findings. The design of the study must be sufficiently powerful to allow the researcher to detect differences that do exist and are relevant to the purpose of the research. A classic design reference for single-subject design research is Hersen and Barlow (1976); Kratochwill (1978) is another source of information about single-N and multiple-N designs. Although this chapter focuses on the analysis of single-subject research, it is important to remember that without a sound design within any research paradigm, the most sophisticated statistics are of little use.

Choices Among Statistical Procedures

There are two classes of statistical analyses: descriptive and inferential. Descriptive statistics simply provide information about the individuals who have been observed; they do not attempt to relate the findings from what was observed to any other group or larger population. This category includes statistics like the mean, mode, and standard deviation. Inferential statistics have a different goal: to make generalizations about the population from which the observations come. That is, inferential statistics attempt to answer the question of whether the observed differences would be the same if the same observations were made with another sample of individuals. Some common inferential statistics are *t* tests, analysis of variance (ANOVA), analysis of covariance (ANCOVA), and regression analysis.

Inferential statistics may be further subdivided into two types: parametric and nonparametric. The examples given in the previous paragraph are parametric statistics—they attempt to estimate characteristics of the larger population based on the characteristics of the observed sample. Nonparametric statistics can be used in situations in which some of the assumptions of statistical analyses cannot be met. For example, *t* tests assume that the population from which the sample was drawn is normally distributed. If there is evidence that the population was not normally distributed, it may be that the results derived from *t* tests on a sample will *not* be applicable, in general, to the population. Two common nonparametric statistics are randomization tests and Cochran's test. There are many others, each designed for specific situations.

Special Problems in Analysis of Single-Subject Data

The most important problem in the analysis of single-subject data is the issue of *serial dependency*, also called *autocorrelation*. Data are said to be serially dependent if the value of a data point is predictable from the data in the series. For example, in the series 1, 2, 3..., the numbers are serially dependent, since each number is predictable from the number immediately preceding it. On the other hand, the data in the series 2, 1, 3... are not serially dependent, since each number is not predictable from its predecessor.

Autocorrelation is often problematic because many statistical procedures assume that the data being analyzed are independently obtained. The assumptions underlying analysis of variance or *t* tests, for example, include such a premise. That is, if one piece of data can be predicted from the other pieces of data, the results of an analysis of variance, or *t* test may produce spurious *F* or *t* ratios. Usually, it is the case that there will be more findings of significant differences when the independence assumption is violated. In some instances, there are corrections that are applied to the statistical procedures to address the problem.

Clearly, it is important to know whether data are autocorrelated. To illustrate the principle underlying this notion, the data in Table 5.1 provide

Example 1: No lag	4	5	6	7	8	9	10	11
	4	5	6	7	8	9	10	11
Example 2: Lag = 1	4	5	6	7	8	9	10	11
	5	6	7	8	9	10	11	4
Example 3: Lag = 2	4	5	6	7	8	9	10	11
	6	7	8	9	10	11	4	5

an example of the concepts of autocorrelation. In the first example, a series of hypothetical measurements are given. These data are paired with
themselves. If we were to calculate a correlation between these two sets, it
would be a perfect correlation, $r = 1.0$. The second example shows the same
data paired by "lagging" the values. Note that the second value is paired
with the first, the third with the second, and so forth. This is referred to as
a *lag 1* autocorrelation. In the third example, a *lag 2* series is given. If the
data are predictable from other elements in the series, they are said to be autocorrelated at a given lag. The use of Bartlett's Test (r) to calculate autocorrelation is relatively simple (a step-by-step procedure for calculating r is
given in Krishef, 1991, p. 58). In short, this procedure will indicate whether
the data violate the independence assumption made by some statistical tests.
If those assumptions are violated, alternative statistical tests may be used.
Randomization tests, discussed later in the chapter, are also choices when
autocorrelations are present.

Autocorrelation can be calculated for any lag, but usually the calculation at lag 1 is sufficient for the analysis of serial dependence problems
in most behavioral research. Kazdin (1984, p. 288ff.) presents details of
methods to perform a finer analysis using different lags on the same data.
He uses a graph of the autocorrelation as a function of the lag to analyze the
extent of serial dependence in the data.

If the data to be analyzed are not significantly autocorrelated, most
statistical tests may be appropriate, providing the other assumptions underlying them are not violated by the conditions of the study. If the data

are autocorrelated, several methods can be employed to transform the data (details of these methods are also given in Krishef, 1991, p. 118ff.). An alternative would be to use a statistic that does not make assumptions that are violated when the data are autocorrelated. Many nonparametric statistics fall in this category. It is important to note that the problem of autocorrelated data is not trivial, since they can produce artifactual interpretations even in the visual analysis of data as well as in the more obvious case of statistical analysis.

Examples of Analysis of Single-Subject Data

Visual Analysis

One of the principles taught in basic statistics is that it is always important to generate a visual display of data (such as interactions, for example) in order to understand what is occurring. Although statistical tests will reveal whether the patterns in the data are significant, they usually do not reveal the patterns that might be readily visible in a graph or other representation of the data.

Parsonson and Baer (1992) present a detailed account of the various ways in which visual analysis or graphing of data can be accomplished. They also discuss current research on the utility of these methods and suggest two other works—Tufte (1983) and (1990)—that present the principles underlying graphic representation of data. The discussion that follows here attempts to outline the important uses of visual analysis in single-subject research. Parsonson and Baer summarize these in six points: visual analysis (1) is quick to yield conclusions and hypotheses, (2) does not require a great deal of technology, (3) can be adapted to a wide range of formats, (4) does not require the researcher to have extensive training for it to be accessible, (5) does not transform the data excessively, and (6) makes few underlying theoretical assumptions (Parsonson & Baer, pp. 16–17).

What sorts of questions can be addressed through the use of graphs? The hypothetical data in Figure 5.1 provide some illustrations. It is clear from a quick examination of the graph that there is certainly a difference between the behavior involved in reading words in context compared with reading words in isolation. It also seems apparent that while there is some variation between the scores on individual occasions, there does not seem to be a consistent difference between different administrations of the context assessment or between different administrations of the isolation assessment. Although we do not have the precise statistical assignment of probability, it is clear that there is no overlap between the two conditions and that the conditions are relatively consistent.

Figure 5.1

**Performance on Words in Context versus Words in Isolation as a
Function of Time in an A-B-A-B Design for a Single Case**

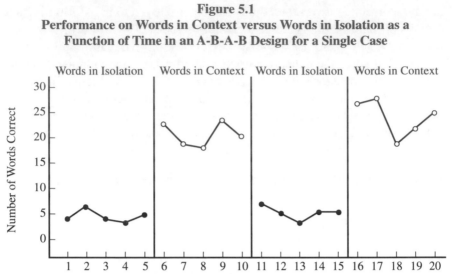

Other sorts of determinations that can be made using visual inspec-
tions include changes from a baseline behavior, changes in trend, and
amount of variability in a set of observations. Although all of these can
also be analyzed by using statistical procedures, it is often useful to have a
visual display for quick analysis. Busk and Marascuilo (1992) discuss the
addition of randomization tests (which are discussed later in this chapter) to
supplement visual analysis. Details of procedures can be found in Wampold
and Furlong (1981) for single-case studies and in Marascuilo and Busk
(1988) for replicated single-case studies.

Parametric Analysis

Linear regression analysis. Another supplement to visual analysis of
graphs—or a replacement for it—is the analysis of the slope of the plot of
data using a linear regression or least-squares analysis. A simple set of calculations can provide an estimate of the "best fit" straight line through the
data. Parsonson and Baer (1992) cite research that suggests that the use of
these lines alters judgments of the data. They posit that the addition of trend
lines may increase the similarity between different judges' interpretation
of data and that the presence of trend lines increases judges' confidence in
their decisions. However, Skiba, Deno, Marston, and Casey (1989) suggest that judges may come to depend on the trend lines and ignore differ-

ences in the data when making interpretations. Parsonson and Baer suggest the need for additional research on this issue.

It is also important to note that use of linear regression techniques (for visual trend lines) introduces another assumption—that the data are best described by a straight line. Alternative solutions that transform or adjust the data to account for nonlinearity are available. The details of some calculations involved in this sort of analysis are clearly and concisely given in Krishef (1991, p. 47ff.).

Ascertaining reasons for differences between scores. Researchers today commonly use multiple measures to assess literacy, but how do we know when two scores are "really" different? How do we know if they differ only by chance? For example, suppose we assess a reader with some word-recognition measure and with a comprehension measure. Clearly, these measures might be—and often are—different: they are not perfectly reliable and they do not correlate perfectly with each other. Since this is the case, it might be that we have an "unusual" score on one measure and a "typical" score on the other. What we need to know is how to determine this.

Payne and Jones (1969) provide a detailed account of the statistical methods involved in determining the answers to questions related to these concerns. They ask three questions:

1. How "abnormal" is a difference between two measures of the same behavior?

2. How large must a difference between two scores be for it to be outside the differences produced by the standard error of measurement for the two tests?

3. How large a difference between two measures will be required to be outside the range of differences found in a control group that has not been subjected to the same interventions?

For the first case, about the abnormality of differences between two scores, Payne and Jones (1969) suggest converting the differences to standard scores and using the normal curve percentile equivalents to determine how frequently the difference would occur in the standardizing population. This method requires that we know the standard deviations of the two tests in a standardizing population and the correlations between the two tests. Although this requirement seems stringent, such information is often available for standardized measures of reading or for other standardized assessments.

The second case, where we wish to know if there is a discrepancy between two scores, involves calculating the standard error of measurement and using it to convert differences between two scores to normal score equivalents, and then to percentiles. This method requires that we know the reliability for the two measures. For standardized measures, these data are often available; for nonstandardized measures, they can often be readily calculated, even though this may involve collecting additional data.

In the third case, where we want to know if the difference between a test and retests is outside the "chance" levels, we can use linear regression to make predictions about the scores. This method requires data on other, nonintervention individuals who simply take the test and a retest. Knowing the correlation between the test and retest scores, as well as the means and standard deviations, will allow the calculation of standard scores that can easily be converted into percentiles.

It is important to note that none of these three techniques dictates the level at which one can make the decision that the scores are not due to chance. For example, in the last example above, a researcher might find that the difference between two scores was such that only 5 percent of all persons taking the test and retest would have so large a difference. The researcher must decide whether the percentile score has any practical significance and set a probability level that it represents an important level of difference.

The three techniques just described involve the use of scores for which some psychometric data are available. They address the reliability question mentioned in the previous section, and they are relatively simple to apply once data are available. They allow the researcher to answer three common questions asked about single cases in research. For nonresearchers, these three methods illustrate simple analytic techniques that should be understood to appreciate single-subject research fully. It is often these sorts of questions that are asked in clinical situations, for example.

The use of t *tests and analysis of variance.* Depending on the design of the study and the types of measures involved, the use of *t* tests or analyses of variance can be appropriate to demonstrate statistical significance between the conditions. There are two basic designs in which this might be the case: A-B-A and A-B-A-B, where A represents the baseline conditions and B represents the intervention or experimental conditions. If the research questions to be answered were about the differences between the baseline and the intervention, a *t* test between all the A observations and all the B observations would be an obvious choice. If the questions were about the trends across all four conditions (in an A-B-A-B design), an ANOVA would be appropriate. However, a problem arises here, as indicated earlier, in that both of these statistical procedures assume that data are independently sampled. That is, the individual pieces of data should not be predictable from one another.

To determine whether the data may be analyzed with one of these statistical procedures, autocorrelations need to be calculated within each phase. (Autocorrelations across the conditions may confound different serial dependencies, so the data should not be analyzed as a whole. Autocorrelations in one phase might cancel out autocorrelations in another, leading to the conclusion that the data were not serially dependent when, in fact, they were.) When the data are not significantly autocorrelated, either t tests or ANOVAS can be applied. If autocorrelations are significant, either different procedures must be used or some sort of transformation of the data must be carried out prior to the analysis.

Another solution to the problem of autocorrelation is offered by Gentile, Roden, and Klein (1972). They suggest aggregating the data from like phases of the study prior to statistical analysis using t test or ANOVAS. By combining the data from the A phases and comparing them with the data from the B phases, serial dependence will be reduced and its effect on the resulting statistical analysis should be diminished. A t test could then be conducted between the A and B phases. If there were more conditions an ANOVA would be appropriate.

In summary, one should use t tests and ANOVAS with caution in analyzing the results of single-subject research. They should be used only after finding no significant autocorrelation in the data. Kazdin (1984, p. 296) suggests that caution needs to be taken in evaluating the means using these tests, pointing out that the trend of the data—the direction and steepness of the slope of the data across observations—is important. Kazdin notes that an accelerated slope would produce scores such that each point was greater than the preceding point. If this were true across both phases, for example, a test between means would be significant. This result might easily be accounted for by the trend in the data rather than by a real difference between conditions.

Time series analysis. A procedure by which data from the different phases of a single-subject study can be compared is called *time series analysis.* Kazdin (1984, p. 296) points out two important features of time series analysis for single-subject research. First, even when there is serial dependency, time series analysis can be used to provide a t test. Time series analyses also provide important information about the trend of behavior across the different conditions of the study. Kazdin lists the separate operations involved in time series analysis as including (1) generating a model for the data, (2) testing its fit to the data, (3) estimating the parameters for the statistic, and (4) generating t tests for level and slope changes. This is obviously not an analysis that can be simply done or summarized. Many computer programs will handle the calculations, after the appropriate thought has gone into the design of the study and the subsequent collection of the data. For more information on specific techniques, a recent, thorough treatment of this topic can be found in McCleary and Welsh (1992). Another helpful source is Glass, Willson, and Gottman (1975).

Nonparametric Analyses

Nonparametric statistical tests, as noted above, do not require any assumption of independence or random selection of samples from a population. It is rare that single-subject research involves randomly selected cases, so these tests are often more appropriate choices than more common parametric analyses.

Randomization tests. The most general of these statistical procedures is the randomization test. (It should be noted that common usage often refers to a large class of tests as randomization tests, although some of them have different names. For example, the Mann–Whitney test is a randomization test performed on ranked data.) In a randomization test, a conventional statistic (like a t or F) is calculated for the data and for repeated orderings of the data. The proportion of significant results is the test statistic used to determine how rarely a test statistic as extreme as the experimental value would result from random assignment alone—that is, as if there were no treatment effect. What this means is that the observed data are analyzed for whatever statistical test is appropriate, anything from totals scores to means to distributions of scores. (Edgington, 1992, notes a number of different possibilities for analyzing data, depending on how many treatments are involved and how they are applied.) The data are then randomized and the statistic is run again, until all the possible combinations have been tested.

If there are many measurement occasions, the number of permutations of the data grows extremely large, thus making calculation burdensome. For example, when there are five treatment observations and five control observations, the number of permutations is 252; for six observations the number is 924; for seven, 3432; and so on. The magnitude of these numbers necessitates intensive calculations, so computer analyses are required. Note also that the randomization test is based on the calculation of other statistics. It compares the frequency of obtaining those statistics from the available data in different orders. This requires calculating the statistic for each of the permutations.

The following is an example of a hypothetical study in which two treatments are used, a control condition and an intervention condition. The data were collected in an A-B-A-B design. For illustration purposes, calculations related only to the first A and B phases are described. In this example, suppose that there are three A observations, followed by five B observations. The scores from each of the conditions are presented in Table 5.2. If the scores were all drawn from a population at random, the possible

Table 5.2
Hypothetical Scores and Arrangements of Scores in an A-B Design

Observed scores for:

Treatment A	14	18	17		
Treatment B:	21	30	27	19	26

	Treatment A			Treatment B					Sum of A scores	Sum of B scores	Sum A minus Sum B
Possible	14	18	17	21	30	19	26	27	49	123	74
orders for	14	17	19	18	21	30	26	27	50	122	72
scores	14	18	19	17	21	30	26	27	51	121	70

number of different arrangements of scores is 56. In this example, the confidence level for rejecting the null hypothesis is set at .05. (Remember that this is an arbitrary decision and it could be set at any value the researcher chooses.) This confidence level means that there are fewer than three outcomes that will occur with a probability of less than .05 (56 x .05 = 2.8). The most extreme arrangements of the data can be chosen by maximizing the difference between the sum of the A scores and the sum of the B scores. The three most extreme outcomes are listed in Table 5.2. If any one of these arrangements is the one found in the data, we can reject the null hypotheses with a probability of a bit more than .05. If the scores in the data do not match one of the extreme arrangements, the null hypothesis cannot be rejected.

The data collected in this example do match one of the extreme cases, allowing the conclusion that the null hypothesis can be rejected. However, if the scores had been arranged slightly differently, it would not have been possible to reject the null hypothesis. For example, suppose the following set of scores had been obtained rather than those shown in Table 5.2.

Treatment A	14	18	21		
Treatment B	17	30	27	19	26

Note that only one score differs in each set. However, the null hypothesis cannot be rejected, since this arrangement is not one of the most extreme.

In this example, the test is assumed to be one tailed. That is, the researcher assumed the results for the intervention would have to be greater than those for the control. If such an assumption had not been possible, then a two-tailed test would have been required, with the most extreme case in either direction representing the critical arrangements. The null hypothesis would be rejected if the obtained set of results were the most extreme or the least extreme case. (Note that since there are three possible orders given the present number of observations and confidence level, it is impossible to divide them into two discrete sets. Using only the most and least extreme case is being conservative, with the actual confidence level being less than .05.)

This logic can be extended for any number of variables, or levels of confidence. If, for example, there had been five observations in each of the two treatment conditions, then there would have been 12 orders that would have allowed the rejection of the null hypothesis. (This calculation is 252 possible orders multiplied by .05, yielding 12.6 orders.). If a confidence level of .01 were chosen, there would be 2 orders (252 x .01 = 2.52) that allow the rejection of the null hypothesis. Although the calculations for a small number of variables and observations can be done by hand, it is not possible to do this efficiently when the number is even at a moderate level. Edgington (1992) deals with the calculation of these tests in more detail and has published a computer program for performing them. Most comprehensive statistical packages, including those available for microcomputers, have routines for calculating a wide range of randomization and nonparametric tests. It is highly recommended that a computer program be used to calculate these statistics when the number of measurements is of even a moderate size.

Some cautions about randomization tests. Some statisticians believe that if the first phase of a research design is a baseline phase, it is inappropriate to use a randomization test, because the randomized design criterion has not been met. They suggest in these cases to exclude the baseline data from the analysis (Suen & Ary, 1989, p. 206).

Edgington (1982) notes that for the randomization-test approach to work, the number of time blocks has to be quite large for the process to be effective. This is a consideration that must be taken into account in the design of the study before data are collected.

Krishef (1991) offers two important cautions against the use of randomization tests. He suggests that randomization tests in general not be used if the treatments produce irreversible behavior. Also, there may be a problem created by the presentation of sequential treatments because of carryover effects. In effect, these problems confound in the data by making it impossible to separate the effects of the treatment from the possible effects of sequence. For example, once a subject has solved a problem that requires a certain type of insight, subsequent attempts at solving that sort of problem will be irretrievably affected. These are important cautions for literacy research, since instructional studies in literacy often do produce effects that are irreversible.

Other nonparametric tests. Edgington (1992, p. 138) recommends that when data are ranked (rather than counted), the Mann–Whitney test is appropriate. If the data are qualitative judgments, Edgington recommends Fisher's Exact Test (p. 139). Other tests that can be used for special situations include the Sign Test, Wilcoxon's Matched Pairs, and Friedman's Analysis of Variance. Wampold and Worsham (1986) have developed a randomization test for multiple-baseline data, and Busk and Marascuilo (1992) have developed a number of tests that can be used when there are replications over subjects. Edgington and Busk and Marascuilo present overviews of these specialized analyses, along with many others.

Two Other Procedures

Ordinal pattern analysis. Thorngate and Carroll (1986) provide a different strategy for the analysis of data from single-subject research. They suggest that since most data analysis in the behavioral sciences is used to detect patterns rather than to make inferences about a population, common inferential statistical procedures may not be appropriate. Further, they suggest that most predictions and observations in behavioral research possess no more than ordinal scale properties. That is, only the order of the scale is important, not the magnitude between the values on the scale. Consequently, many inferential statistical procedures are inappropriate because they assume the data being analyzed have, at least, interval scale properties.

Whether these assumptions are correct or useful is well beyond the scope of the present chapter. An intriguing statement appears in the concluding section of the Thorngate and Carroll (1986) chapter: "In the end it is the pattern of data, not the statistical significance of differences that determines research importance" (p. 230). This perspective is presented as a promising alternative to other analyses (described fully on page 201–231 of their work), when the conditions set forth in the preceding paragraph obtain. There seem to be few published studies using ordinal pattern analysis, so its value is difficult to assess. However, with increased evidence on informal, nonstandardized measures, this approach may become more attractive.

Decision analysis. Bromley (1986) suggests another method of approaching the interpretation and analysis of single-subject data. He applies "decision analysis" to case data. Although he admits that his interest is mostly practical, there seems to be no reason why this analysis could not be applied to research data.

Decision analysis can be thought of as a four-way classification table in which the advantages and disadvantages of a particular action are assessed. Actions are either important or not; they are either likely to occur or not. The following is an example in which the decision might be to have a student participate in a clinical remedial reading treatment. The treatment might have a number of advantages—the child might focus on specific reading activities, receive concentrated tutoring, or have a special set of materials—and some disadvantages—the child might be isolated from other students or not receive instruction in other areas that students in the classroom receive. Still other aspects of the treatment might not have any effect at all: for example, the time of day might be irrelevant. In decision analysis, the advantages and disadvantages would be arranged in a table such as the following:

	More likely	Less likely
More important	A	B
Less important	C	D

Each advantage would be assigned a value of importance and likelihood. For example, focusing on specific reading activities might be more important and more likely, so it would be assigned to the A category. The isolation from the classroom might be less important and more likely, placing it in the C category.

What decision analysis does is focus on the multiple dimensions of a course of action. This is important in reading research, since many different factors work to bring about a single result. Bromley (1986) gives examples in clinical contexts of estimating probabilities associated with each course of action, allowing more precision in the assessment of research results. Again, there are few published research studies using this concept, but there is, in principle, no reason why it could not be applied.

Meta-Analysis

Meta-analysis is a procedure that goes beyond the limits of the conventional analyses described previously. It is often used when researchers want to know how effective a particular treatment was over a wide range of conditions in a number of different studies. One way of finding this out is by calculating effect size (Glass, 1976) for the studies as a group. Effect size is simply a standardized measurement of the difference between the control conditions and the treatment conditions. Thus, scores from different studies using different measures can be compared by converting them to normalized values. Although it has become relatively straightforward to calculate effect sizes for conventional research that includes a control or comparison group, Busk and Serlin (1992) note that this approach is uncommon when dealing with single-subject research. They speculate that this may be because the computations are too difficult or that meta-analysis is simply inappropriate for single-subject data. The possibility of serial dependence in the data makes the application of meta-analytic techniques more difficult. Busk and Serlin provide a detailed account of the ways in which effect-size calculations may be made under a variety of assumptions for single-subject data. Their work provides steps on procedures and an excellent bibliography for extended reading.

Meta-analysis may become more important as the number of researchers interested in single-subject designs increases. As soon as a critical mass of work exists in which similar variables are studied by different researchers in a variety of settings, it becomes important to determine whether there is any consistency across those studies. Meta-analytic techniques should be an increasingly useful way of comparing those results.

Questions to Ask about Statistical Analysis of Single-Subject Data

It is important to note at the outset of this section that questions about statistical analysis of single-subject data cannot be asked in isolation. Questions about design, instrumentation, data coding, and the like all contribute to (or detract from) the value of data analyses. Once again, readers must be cautioned that unless a study is well designed, it cannot be analyzed satisfactorily. Many decisions about design, instruments, subjects, and settings, as well as other issues, affect the choices of statistical procedures in research. The summaries of the various types of statistical procedures touch on some of the considerations.

What follows is an attempt to provide a checklist of questions that research consumers should ask when reading studies involving single-subject designs. Theory (or the lack of it) plays a critical role in all research, not just single-subject research. Consequently, the first of these questions deals directly with this issue, even though some might believe it is a different sort of concern, playing little or no role in statistical analyses.

1. *Did a theory guide the research being reported? If so, what is it? If not, does the author offer a reasonable explanation for not having a theory?* The answer to these questions is important in that it allows the reader to make decisions about the appropriateness of almost all that follows in the study. If a researcher is concerned only with a particular individual, it may not be necessary to have a theory, although the work of Bromley (1986) and Thorngate and Carroll (1986) suggests that a theoretical orientation may be important, even at this level. However, much of the time research intends to determine whether the observed effects in one situation generalize to another. Without examining in detail the variables that make situations unique, it is difficult to generalize. Stressing the importance of theory minimizes the possibility that an author or researcher will ignore these issues.

Finally, a theory guides the researcher to collect certain types of data, and the type of data clearly has an immediate effect on the choice of statistical procedure. If choices concerning data have been made before the study as the result of theoretical speculation, the statistical analyses will be much more powerful.

2. *Do the authors present evidence to show that they have accounted for the special problems of single-subject data if statistical analyses are used? What is the evidence?* These special problems of single-subject research include the design of the study, serial dependency in the data, and small numbers of observations—all of which have been addressed earlier in this chapter. If the authors do not present evidence on these points, they may not have dealt with them, and their results and analyses may not be trustworthy. They may have obtained artifactual results because of some of the assumptions underlying the statistical tests used. This is a strong signal to be wary of the conclusions. It is not, however, a guarantee that something is wrong, merely a warning that it might be.

Kratochwill (1992, p. 5) lists 12 research characteristics that can produce strong or weak inferences about data. The evaluation of the research and the choice of analytic procedures should be influenced by choices along such dimensions as type of data (subjective or objective), assessment occasions (single or repeated), number of subjects (one case or an aggregate of several cases), and impact of the treatment (one or multiple outcome measures). In each case, Kratochwill suggests that the first alternative in each of the examples in the preceding sentence is a "low-inference" choice, while the second is "high inference." Low-inference strategies will lead to weak conclusions beyond the data; high-inference strategies will lead to stronger conclusions. Choices along these dimensions must be made before the study is conducted since no analysis, statistical or other, can be better than the data on which it is based. For example, an imprecise, subjective measure will not be any more accurate after it has been analyzed statistically. Data that are not collected during the study will never be available later on. One cannot return to collect additional data at a later time. In addition, the design of a study will determine what sorts of statistical analyses are appropriate.

3. *Have the authors chosen appropriate analyses in light of the answer to the second question? If so, what are they? Are alternatives discussed? Are the advantages and disadvantages of the selected analyses and the alternatives presented? Did these alternatives include transforming the data?* If so, remember that the conclusions may apply only to the transformed data and not necessarily to the raw data.

When an author chooses a statistical procedure without a clear rationale, the reader must, once again, be wary of the conclusions. The discussions of different procedures presented earlier in the chapter will assist the reader in evaluating decisions that researchers make.

4. *What are the actual results of the statistical analyses?* Of primary importance is whether the authors presented statistical analyses that dealt with autocorrelation or addressed the serial dependence problem in some other way. This is the question that must be asked, since the answer dictates, in large measure, what the authors should have done in their statistical analyses. Obviously, this is related to the third question.

Almost equally important, the reader should be able to list the questions that guided the study, relate them to the findings, and, in turn, relate the findings to some sort of analysis—statistical or otherwise. If this can't be done, one must be a bit skeptical of the results. At the same time, a large number of different statistical tests applied to the same data should also raise a caution. When there are many statistical procedures, some of which do not indicate statistical differences, the author may be manipulating the statistical tests. That is, the author may be on a "fishing expedition," hoping that one of the tests will produce a result consistent with what he or she envisioned at the outset. Look for explicit rationales for each procedure, and maintain a skeptical attitude about those analyses that have no such rationale.

The confidence level is obviously an important concern. Since this is an arbitrary value, selected by the researcher, an appropriate rationale should be provided. As indicated above, the design may have a limiting effect on the choice of levels.

5. *Are the results convincing? Why or why not?* The probability levels, confidence intervals, and the size of the effects that have been found should be clearly given. All other things being equal, the lower the probability that the effects happened by chance, the more confidence one can have in the findings (for example, $p < .01$ usually indicates more confidence that the finding was not by chance than does $p < .05$). Similarly, larger effect sizes should produce more certainty for a reader that the findings are important in the real world, not merely statistically significant.

A special note must be added about the use of graphs and visual analysis to draw conclusions. Technically, visual analysis doesn't fall into the category of statistical analysis. However, it is quite often used to describe the data or assist in interpreting the data. In these cases, readers must be particularly intent on answering this fifth question. Someone looking at Figure 5.1 would not fail to agree that there is a difference between the conditions. Other examples, however, may not be so clear. The reader must be convinced that the conclusions an author reaches, based on visual analysis, are the same as anyone else would reach. The cautions provided earlier in the chapter about the use of visual analysis should be heeded. The best advice is that, whenever possible, visual analysis should be supplemented by statistical analysis.

Summary

This chapter has sketched the considerations that go into selecting, using, and understanding a statistical or other analytic procedure for single-subject research data. It is not possible to become an expert in combining statistical analysis with the more typical visual analysis often used in single-subject research by reading a summary chapter such as this. If, as a reader, you have any doubts about the nature of the analyses, you should attempt to find more information in the sources cited throughout this chapter. Although many of them are technical, they can provide additional information about what to look for in these analyses. The same sources will also provide additional insights into the sorts of conclusions that can be drawn as a result of them.

The special needs of single-subject research require rather specialized methods. There is a critical need to consider the appropriateness of particular designs prior to collection of data to take into account the ultimate statistical analysis. Other specialized statistical techniques range from simple graphing to sophisticated inferential analyses. Each technique has advantages and disadvantages depending on the characteristics of the design and data collected. Each technique makes different assumptions about the purpose of the analysis and the characteristics of the data being analyzed. Through the appropriate use of these analytical tools, researchers can target their problems more specifically. Readers can use this knowledge to become more thoughtful critics and consumers of the research.

References

Bromley, D. (1986). *The case-study method in psychology and related disciplines.* Chichester, UK: John Wiley & Sons.

Busk, P., & Marascuilo, L. (1992). Statistical analysis in single-case research: Issues, procedures, and recommendations with applications to multiple behaviors. In T. Kratochwill & J. Levin (Eds.), *Single-case research design and analysis: New directions for psychology and education* (pp. 159-186). Hillsdale, NJ: Erlbaum.

Busk, P., & Serlin, R. (1992). Meta-analysis for single-case research. In T. Kratochwill & J. Levin (Eds.), *Single-case research design and analysis: New directions for psychology and education* (pp. 187–212). Hillsdale, NJ: Erlbaum.

Edgington, E. (1982). Non-parametric tests for single-subject multiple schedule experiments. *Behavioral Assessment, 4,* 83–91.

Edgington, E. (1992). Non-parametric tests for single-case experiments. In T. Kratochwill & J. Levin (Eds.), *Single-case research design and analysis: New directions for psychology and education* (pp. 133–157). Hillsdale, NJ: Erlbaum.

Gentile, J., Roden, A., & Klein, R. (1972). Analysis of variance model for the intrasubject replication design. *Journal of Applied Behavior Analysis, 5,* 193–198.

Glass, G. (1976). Primary, secondary, and meta-analysis of research. *Review of Research in Education, 5*, 351–379.

Glass, G., Willson, B., & Gottman, J. (1975). *Design and analysis of time series experiments.* Boulder, CO: Colorado Associated University Press.

Hersen, M., & Barlow, D.H. (1976). *Single case experimental designs: Strategies for studying behavior change.* New York: Pergamon.

Kazdin, A.E. (1976). Statistical analyses for single-case experimental designs. In M. Hersen & D.H. Barlow (Eds.), *Single case experimental designs: Strategies for studying behavior change* (pp. 265–316). New York: Pergamon.

Kazdin, A. (1984). Statistical analyses for single-case experimental designs. In D.H. Barlow & M. Hersen (Eds.), *Single case experimental designs: Strategies for studying behavior change* (2nd ed.). New York: Pergamon.

Kratochwill, T.R. (Ed.). (1978). *Single subject research: Strategies for evaluating change.* New York: Academic.

Kratochwill, T.R. (1992). Single-case research design and analysis: An overview. In T. Kratochwill & J. Levin (Eds.), *Single-case research design and analysis: New directions for psychology and education* (pp. 1–14). Hillsdale, NJ: Erlbaum.

Krishef, C. (1991). *Fundamental approaches to single subject design and analysis.* Malabar, FL: Krieger.

Marascuilo, L., & Busk, P. (1988). Combining statistics for multiple-baseline AB and replicated ABAB designs across subjects. *Behavioral Assessment, 10*, 1–28.

McCleary, R., & Welsh, W. (1992). Philosophical and statistical foundations of time-series experiments. In T. Kratochwill & J. Levin (Eds.), *Single-case research design and analysis: New directions for psychology and education* (pp. 41–91). Hillsdale, NJ: Erlbaum.

Mudre, L.H., & McCormick, S. (1989). Effects of meaning-focused cues on underachieving readers' context use, self-corrections, and literal comprehension. *Reading Research Quarterly, 24*, 89–113.

Palincsar, A.S., & Brown, A.L. (1984). Reciprocal teaching of comprehension-fostering and comprehension-monitoring activities. *Cognition & Instruction, 1*, 117–175.

Parsonson, B., & Baer, D.M. (1992). The visual analysis of data and current research into the stimuli controlling it. In T. Kratochwill & J. Levin (Eds.), *Single-case research design and analysis: New directions for psychology and education* (pp. 15–40). Hillsdale, NJ: Erlbaum.

Payne, H., & Jones, H. (1969). Statistics for the investigation of individual cases. In P. Davidson & P. Costello (Eds.), *N = 1: Experimental studies of single cases* (pp. 46–58). New York: Van Nostrand.

Skiba, R., Deno, S., Marston, D., & Casey, A. (1989). Influence of trend estimation and subject familiarity on practitioners' judgments of intervention effectiveness. *Journal of Special Education, 22*, 433–446.

Suen, H., & Ary, D. (1989). *Analyzing quantitative behavioral observation data.* Hillsdale, NJ: Erlbaum.

Thorngate, W., & Carroll, B. (1986). Ordinal pattern analysis. In J. Valsiner (Ed.), *The individual subject and scientific psychology* (pp. 201–231). New York: Plenum.

Tufte, E. (1983). *The visual display of quantitative information.* Cheshire, CT: Graphics Press.

Tufte, E. (1990). *Envisioning information.* Cheshire, CT: Graphics Press.

Wampold, B., & Furlong, M. (1981). Randomization tests in single-subject designs: Illustrative examples. *Journal of Behavioral Assessment, 3*, 329–341.

Wampold, B., & Worsham, N. (1986). Randomization tests for multiple-baseline designs. *Behavioral Assessment, 8*, 135–143.

Statistical Analysis Procedures   103

CHAPTER 6

Combining Single-Subject Experimental Designs with Qualitative Research

Tanja L. Bisesi
Taffy E. Raphael

This chapter offers the literacy researcher an alternative strategy in research. In contrast to other chapters, here we focus on combining two approaches: single-subject experimental and case-study qualitative research. In general, single-subject experimental researchers are interested in analyzing quantitatively the effect of an intervention on one or more learning outcomes, while qualitative researchers focus on generating narrative descriptions and interpretations of phenomena (for example, learning events, attitudes, or behaviors) that occur without explicit interventions. These two research approaches are described by some as opposing (Hersh, 1990) because of long-standing debates between quantitative researchers with whom single-subject researchers are sometimes associated and qualitative or descriptive researchers, associated with the case-study approach. The debate has centered on both identifying the phenomena most important to study and determining how best to study them.

In this chapter we first highlight the contrasting features of single-subject and case-study research, using one example of each. Second, we examine the quantitative-qualitative debate, foreshadowing aspects to consider when combining methods. In the final section, we propose advantages of combining research designs, within the context of cautions highlighted by the quantitative-qualitative debate. Our goal is to offer a disciplined yet optimistic perspective regarding the potential of merging quantitative and qualitative research methods. We had originally hoped to organize the chapter using numerous examples of studies that had successfully merged single-subject with case-study methods. Yet despite using a range of search strategies, we had difficulty locating examples. We hope this chapter sheds light on the question of why more researchers have not combined methods as well as on how such methods can be successfully combined.

Features of Single-Subject and Case-Study Research

Although single-subject and case-study approaches share an emphasis on research with individuals rather than larger populations, the traditions from which they arise result in inquiry capable of addressing different types of research questions in different ways. As Table 6.1 suggests, single-subject experimental research and case-study qualitative research differ on aspects of assumptions, research design, and research procedures. The assumptions, drawn from the research paradigm's parent discipline, include beliefs about the world and scientific knowledge. Research design issues deal with how to set up research (purpose, questions, settings), while research procedure issues address how to collect, analyze, and judge the value of data.

To highlight the differences between these two approaches, the following section describes the assumptions, research design, and procedures of two literacy studies—one conducted using a single-subject experimental design and the other employing a case-study, qualitative design.

Single-Subject Experimental Design

Mudre and McCormick (1989) conducted a study with a single-subject experimental design to examine the effects of a meaning-focused cue intervention on context use, self-corrections, and literal comprehension of early elementary underachieving readers. They also investigated whether the effects were maintained after the intervention ended and the extent to which the parents carried out the intervention they were taught to employ.

Assumptions. Mudre and McCormick's study focused on effects: specifically, they were interested in determining the effect of a parent-tutoring intervention on parent and student behaviors. This research goal assumes that there are relatively stable, identifiable, and measurable relationships between the causes and effects of literacy learning. It also assumes that by understanding functional relationships, visible laws of literacy learning can be discerned and built on to establish new knowledge about literacy development.

Design. In this investigation, Mudre and McCormick applied a single-subject design to test and verify four hypotheses to determine whether (1)

Table 6.1
Characteristics of Single-Subject Experimental and Case-Study Designs

Aspect of Comparison	Single-Subject Experimental Designs	Case-Study Designs
Fundamental Assumptions:		
Parent Discipline	Psychology	Anthropology/sociology
Beliefs about the world (i.e., ontology)	Reality is stable and inherent in the physical world	Reality is multifaceted and open to interpretation
Beliefs about knowledge (i.e., epistemology)	Scientific knowledge is made up of "facts" and "laws" that rule human learning and behavior and build on knowledge that has been discovered previously	Scientific knowledge consists of different "interpretations" of human learning and behavior, each limited by its unique perspective but contributing to some holistic and evolving understanding
Research Design:		
Purpose	Prediction and verification: "hypothesis testing"	Description, explanation, and understanding: "hypothesis generating":
Types of questions	Do/does? Is/are? Can?	What? How? Why?
Settings	Controlled	Naturalistic
Research Procedures:		
Type of data	Objective, resulting in numerical outcomes	Interpretive, resulting in description
Data collection	Standardized measurement	Interpretation by researcher(s)
Analysis	Deductive/hypothesis grounded	Inductive/data grounded
Validity concerns	Internal validity (control); external validity (generalizability)	Internal validity (common sense); ecological validity (applicability to "real" settings)
Integrity/reliability	Replication	Negotiation and triangulation

Bisesi & Raphael

the intervention would facilitate development of certain strategies and abilities in young, underachieving readers; (2) readers' parents could be taught to provide feedback that would result in the desired effects; (3) the training effects would be durable for both parents and young readers over time; and (4) the reading effect would transfer across texts.

To test these hypotheses, it was necessary to create controlled instructional conditions—that is, experimental procedures for eliminating extraneous variables in a study. Although they incorporated aspects of experimental group design (such as statistically analyzing student effects and parent feedback data), these researchers also examined their data through a multiple-baseline design (see Chapter 3 of this volume). Parent training of each feedback type (such as self-correction, context use, verbal praise) was initiated sequentially and measured across five-day periods during the study. Parents served as their own controls.

Procedures. Mudre and McCormick's procedures were deductive, beginning with specific hypotheses and followed by collecting data to support or refute the cause-effect assumptions. They demonstrated the paramount concern of most single-subject researchers—the ability to establish functional relationships (see Chapter 1). That is, the researchers were interested in controlling the intervention context, thus reducing the chance of competing explanations for observed effects (such as parents' use of a tutoring strategy, students' use of strategies) within a multiple-baseline design.

Mudre and McCormick's study also examined whether these results could be generalized by measuring the degree to which effects transferred across reading tasks. They addressed the issue of user satisfaction by collecting survey information on participants' attitudes regarding the intervention (asking, for example, whether consumers were satisfied with the intervention's goals, procedures, and results). And finally, they used standardized measures and quantitative criteria to describe and select young readers and reading materials, to evaluate the integrity of observations (such as interrater agreements in categorizing parent and student behaviors), and to document the effects of intervention.

Case-Study Design

In contrast to a single-subject experimental approach, Goatley, Brock, and Raphael (1993) adopted a case-study design to examine how diverse learners (bilingual, special education, and regular education students) participated in literature discussions called "book clubs" that took place within the context of a classroom reading program. The researchers focused on understanding aspects of the classroom setting, the participants, and the group interactions within a student-led response group. The stated goal of the study was "to better understand the successes and frustrations of diverse learners within regular education classroom response groups" (p. 3).

Assumptions. Goatley, Brock, and Raphael's concern for understanding multiple and personal perspectives (such as their own, the teacher's, and the students') on the literacy learning experience suggests a belief that there are no objective facts or laws about literacy learning that can be discovered, only numerous interpretations that contribute to some evolving whole. For example, these researchers focused on students' interpretations of taught strategies in relationship to the researchers' interpretation of what was taught, which lead to a holistic and evolving understanding of a learning phenomenon. This contrasts with the Mudre and McCormick study, which focused on the effects of taught strategies on literacy behavior to establish intervention principles. Thus, from the perspective of Goatley et al., scientific knowledge consists of multiple and equally valid interpretations, rather than discoverable laws.

Design. In contrast to experimental designs derived from the hard sciences, the case-study design grew up within the disciplines of anthropology and sociology. Goatley et al. used a case-study design to generate rich and complex descriptions (of participants, of literacy learning experiences) and explanations (of how norms and roles were developed within the group) to develop understanding (how diverse learners participate in literature discussion groups), rather than to establish cause-effect relationships. They also used this design to generate hypotheses such as that diverse learners can participate effectively in a regular education setting within the context of literature discussion groups. In contrast, Mudre and McCormick (1989) tested their hypotheses.

Rather than focusing on effects, Goatley et al.'s research questions looked at the process: (1) how the discussion group provides opportunities for diverse learners to participate and what roles/relationships are established within the group; (2) what norms develop within the group for participation and how they relate to whole-class norms; and (3) within the discussion group, what opportunities there are for diverse learners to develop and use text interpretation strategies.

Procedures. To answer their questions, Goatley et al. applied observational procedures (such as field notes and audiotapes of discussion) and interview techniques within the context of the classroom to develop a sense of what occurred "naturally" without their explicit involvement. This focus reflects the case-study researcher's primary concern with ecological validity, or the desire to find out what happens in an instructional context, rather than with the potential effects of an intervention, which was the focus of Mudre and McCormick's study.

Goatley et al. used a variety of data-collection procedures typical of qualitative work, including standardized procedures (such as written questionnaires and formal interviews) and open-ended strategies (such as participant observation and informal interview). No measurement such as standardized test scores was used to select or describe students. Instead, Goatley et al. used lengthy, narrative descriptions to characterize their participants.

In contrast to numerical data to describe the significance of an intervention, Goatley et al. used formats typical of narrative description and excerpts of raw data such as actual dialogue between students. They generated patterns inductively from their data (such as leadership patterns within the group). Patterns were not predicted before data were collected and examined, but emerged as the researchers read, reread, and talked about data from field notes, interviews, questionnaires, and discussion transcripts. They also used extended excerpts of raw data to illustrate identified patterns and confirmed the patterns through triangulation of data sources, looking at different sources of data to determine if they led to similar conclusions, and at researcher negotiation to obtain consistency in judgment.

Finally, conclusions and explanations of findings were based on common sense. Explanations proposed by Goatley et al. concerning the nature of diverse students' interactions within response groups as well as their roles and interpretations were presented in terms of logical argument. Consequently, in contrast to establishing cause-and-effect relationships as in Mudre and McCormick, this case study generated conclusions based on reason and supported by direct evidence on the processes of interaction.

Relevant Issues of the Quantitative-Qualitative Debate

As is obvious from the examples above, single-subject and case-study research approaches clearly derive from different research traditions. We believe that researchers should be aware of and seriously reflect on the issues raised by the ongoing debate on their respective merits. Relevant aspects of this debate have roots reaching back more than 300 years, as shown in Table 6.2. Major issues that have created controversy and are important to understand before the approaches can be successfully combined include (1) what constitutes data, (2) how data should be collected, and (3) the nature of knowledge. In this section, we discuss the historical roots of the current controversy along with issues to consider when combining methodologies.

What Counts as Data?

In the mid-17th century, John Graunt, a British merchant, and Hermann Conrig, a German professor (see Rizo, 1991) debated how de-

Table 6.2
Timeline of Significant Events and People in the Quantitative-Qualitative Debate

	17th Century	19th Century	Early 20th Century	Late 20th Century
Events:	Debate over value of birth and death figures versus narrative descriptions for understanding aspects of society	Arguments over the "science" of social learning and behavior—whether to ground in natural sciences or create new social science	Debate over beliefs about knowledge: Is it fixed, real, objective or changing, constructed, interpreted?	Kuhn introduces his concept of paradigm: there are no universal truths
Focus of debate:	Methodology: What counts as data?	Methodology: What counts as "scientific" procedure?	Epistemology: What is knowledge?	Purism or pragmatism: Should alternative paradigms be combined?
Key contributors:				
Quantitative	Graunt	Comte, Mill	*Vienna Circle* (Carnap, Hempel, Schlick, Ayer)	
Qualitative	Conrig	Dilthey, Windelband	*Chicago School* (Mead, Burgess, Thomas)	
Purists				Eisner, Erickson, Rist
Pragmatists				Gage, Huberman, Miles
"Practicalists"				Cherryholmes, Eisenhart, Fredericks, Garrison, Howe, Miller

Bisesi & Raphael

scriptions of society could provide a meaningful analysis of their social world, taking different approaches and ultimately questioning the validity of each other's research (see Table 6.2). Graunt valued numerical representations of measurable aspects of society (such as the numbers of births and deaths that occurred in a specific period of time) and created the first life and mortality tables, while Conrig thought the valuable information to describe concerned the state as a whole—its laws, its purposes as a political body, and so forth. Such information required in-depth, narrative description. These two approaches reveal the long-standing differences between quantitative and qualitative views of what counts as "data," differences we still debate, discuss, and question.

What Counts as "Scientific" Procedure?

Over the next two centuries, these methodological debates expanded to consider how evidence should be gathered based on different perspectives about the relationship between the natural and the social sciences (Rizo, 1991). During the 19th century, researchers such as Auguste Comte and John Stuart Mill suggested that the social sciences were akin to the natural sciences and, thus, should draw upon scientific methodologies. They argued that there were underlying laws for human behavior just as there were such laws for the behaviors of physical objects. From this perspective, one of the primary tasks of the researcher was to develop a controlled experiment that would reveal the workings of these laws. Thus, research methodologies required clear designs that gathered data on baseline behaviors, intervention, and measurable outcomes.

In contrast to the experimental tradition of that time was the position assumed by social researchers such as Wilhelm Dilthey and W. Windelband (Rizo, 1991). These researchers argued that since the social sciences fundamentally differed from the "hard" sciences, they required a new methodology characterized by observation of social interactions within natural settings. They questioned the existence of stable and discoverable "laws" of human learning and behavior. The goal of such research was to generate hypotheses that could describe, explain, or lead to understanding of such behavior.

What Counts as Knowledge?

From the 17th until the 19th century, the debate continued to center around the nature of data and how they were gathered. By the early 20th century, the debate expanded to the philosophical realm, as social—and, specifically, educational—researchers began to argue the nature of knowledge itself: Was it a concrete, stable, measurable given waiting to be uncovered, or a construction interpreted within a particular social and cultural context, influenced by history and the particular individuals involved? These two perspectives were most visible in two groups of 20th century researchers: the Vienna Circle and the Chicago School.

The Vienna Circle consisted of Austrian and German scientists from a range of disciplinary backgrounds such as mathematics, philosophy, and history. They argued that knowledge was meaningful only if it was objective and could be proven empirically—that is, at least two people must see and therefore be able to verify a phenomenon (Phillips, 1983). Such beliefs lent themselves to quantification and the experimental procedures of the natural sciences. In contrast, the Chicago School drew on anthropology, sociology, and the other humanities in deciding what were valued as data, collection procedures, and knowledge (Rizo, 1991). First, these researchers assumed that the world was not governed by stable laws of learning and behavior—which they believed were complex and constantly changing—and accurate predictions could therefore not be made. Second, even if the world were stable, researchers could never know its laws directly because every person interprets the world through the lens of their prior experiences and beliefs. Since knowledge could not be judged or verified in any objective way, these researchers believed it should be judged by whether it "made sense." The belief that knowledge was subjective led the Chicago School to value in-depth, narrative accounts of personal, spontaneous experiences over numerical summaries of behaviors that were predicted and verified under controlled circumstances.

How Can Research Paradigms Be Combined?

In the last half of the 20th century, researchers have begun to question whether it is possible to identify a single best methodology. Philosophers such as Kuhn (1962) suggested there are no universal truths about learning and behavior in any area; rather, our views of the world are determined by the paradigms within which we operate, the unique combination of beliefs about the world, knowledge, and methods of research that determine the ways researchers collect and interpret data. The debate in the research field has now shifted from identifying the best method for research to recognizing that different paradigms lead to different understandings.

Questions have emerged about combining methods from different paradigms, with three positions taken: (1) purist, (2) pragmatist, and (3) "practicalist." Purists (see, for example, Eisner, 1991; Erickson, 1986; Rist, 1977, 1980) believe that philosophical assumptions dictate methodological choices such as research questions, types of data, and collection procedures and, therefore, different research paradigms or approaches are incompatible and should not be combined. Pragmatists (see Gage, 1989; Miles & Huberman, 1984), on the other hand, believe that there is no inherent link between philosophical assumptions and methodology and advocate blending aspects of all paradigms without condition, toward the pragmatic purpose of improving peoples' lives. We identify with the third group—the "practicalists" such as Cherryholmes (1992), Garrison (1986), Howe (1985; Howe & Eisenhart, 1990), and Miller and Fredericks (1991)—who believe that practical wisdom and logic should guide the development of coherent research approaches. Thus, to combine methods effectively, it helps to know the aspects of the debate.

Combining Single-Subject and Case-Study Research

When we decide to combine elements of single-subject and case-study research, how should we think about merging the different views? We draw on issues raised by the quantitative-qualitative debate to provide insights and guidance, including (1) assumptions, goals, and questions, (2) the nature of appropriate research design and procedures, and (3) the nature of legitimate research data.

Assumptions. Single-subject experimental researchers provide us with prescriptive information about the intervention effects on particular students, while case-study researchers contribute to our understanding of individuals' experiences and interpretations. Single-subject researchers believe that predictable cause-effect relationships can be established, while case-study researchers believe that any identified casual relationship is transient and incomplete. To combine methods into coherent sets of alternative research goals, questions, and strategies, we believe it critical that researchers first establish the primary paradigm within which they are working, and shape their study accordingly. While we do not believe that research methods should be dictated by philosophical assumptions, we do believe that sensible design and methodological choices must be guided by the researchers' principal assumptions, goals, and questions. Since the goals and questions of primary concern to those working within a single-subject experimental paradigm focus on determining the intervention effects, that emphasis should define the overall design and regulate the selection of methods.

Research design and procedures. After establishing basic assumptions, goals, and research questions and choosing a guiding paradigm, the next step in combining approaches is to designate a primary research design. For single-subject researchers, this would involve selecting the most appropriate single-subject design (see Chapters 2, 3, and 4 in this volume) for examining the intervention of interest. Case-study methodologies (such as interviews, participant observation) could be incorporated to strengthen and build the coherence of the general design of the study. These methods could be used to address critical questions such as how the study was implemented, the context within which it was implemented, or the nature of students' attitudes and responses during intervention. These methods, however, should be carefully employed to add insight to the study, and not to lead it in tangential and unproductive directions.

Research data. To effectively combine case-study methods with single-subject designs, researchers will need to broaden their definitions of what counts as legitimate data and how they can be represented. Single-subject experimental methods are respected for their ability to measure interventions and their effects objectively and quantitatively. To reap the benefits of case-study methods in combination with single-subject methods, we must respect more subjective data such as interview responses and narrative descriptions. Such qualitative data could be used to support quantitative definitions of "baseline" or "effects," and could be triangulated with quantitative data to strengthen anticipated results or help to explain the unanticipated.

Advantages to Single-Subject–Case-Study Combination Designs

Applying case-study methods within the context of a single-subject study could enhance the study of an intervention's effects. The ultimate worth of any intervention study, however, is the difference it can make to those people who might be involved in applying the findings. The worth aspect of an intervention study is referred to as its *social validity*. Evidence of social validity establishes the importance or acceptability of intervention programs from a societal perspective (Geller, 1991) and their subsequent likelihood of being applied. This term was first introduced by Wolf (1978), who suggested that intervention studies be socially validated on at least three levels: (1) the significance of their goals, (2) the appropriateness of their procedures, and (3) the importance of their effects. Wolf (1978) also suggested that the social validation process be accomplished through the collection of subjective, qualitative information (such as subjects' attitude toward the intervention), implying a potentially powerful role for case-study methodologies within the context of a single-subject design.

The most common form of social validity assessment involves collecting qualitative information on consumer satisfaction. For example, Mudre and McCormick's study (1989) gathered individual survey data to evaluate participants' attitudes toward the program and its perceived effectiveness. Studies on such interventions as Reading Recovery (Clay, 1979) might also benefit from the collection of qualitative data. Questionnaires from principals, teachers, students, and parents about their level of satisfaction with the program, for example, could provide insight into the perceived acceptability and importance of the program, guiding program modifications and contributing to its successful implementation in other contexts. The goal of this type of data collection is to discover the level of satisfaction of the participants, since that reflects the potential for both acceptability and importance of any intervention. Other case-study methods such as in-depth personal interviews with participants and individual "needs" surveys collected from people who would potentially be applying the study's results could also be integrated into the single-subject design.

Some intervention researchers have argued for a priority to be placed on collection of more quantitative and objective evidence of an intervention's value or social validity, such as using data on how "normal" individuals perform on a factor of interest to establish outcome competency levels (e.g., Van Houten, 1979; Winett, Moore, & Anderson, 1991). Although we believe that quantitative data should be considered, qualitative data, nevertheless, remain a cornerstone of sound social-validity assessment (as in Geller, 1991; Schwartz & Baer, 1991), and their integration into single-subject experimental designs can offer a wealth of information.

Once the importance of an intervention and its effects have been established, other aspects of the intervention should be evaluated before considering future implementation. Evidence collected and used to judge an intervention's application potential fall into the following three categories: (1) procedural integrity or reliability, (2) internal validity, and (3) external validity.

Integrity

Procedural or treatment integrity is the ability to measure a skill or trait or implement a given treatment consistently across time, setting, subject, judge, or teacher. Researchers want to make sure that they are implementing the same intervention and measuring the same outcomes across subjects and over time to draw appropriate conclusions about treatment effects. Although single-subject researchers typically ensure treatment and procedural integrity by precisely and quantitatively defining the intervention before the training period begins, this will not necessarily guarantee consistency during implementation.

Incorporating case-study methods within the context of a single-subject design could provide valuable documentation and additional evidence of integrity. These methods may complement procedures typically used by single-subject experimental researchers in assessing the integrity of independent variables. For example, researchers analyzing the influence of strategy training on student metacognition could collect in-depth descriptions of intervention contexts and outcomes in the form of field notes, providing detailed documentation of exactly how the treatment was implemented with particular students or groups of students and what the results were. Case-study techniques that could be useful here include collecting field notes, documenting the implementation and its results, and in-depth interviews about the specifics of the procedures. Such information about interventions and outcome skills would allow investigators potentially to detect and control the implementation of the intervention across different contexts. We believe that qualitative data resulting from these methods would make consistent replication of the intervention by other researchers and educators easier and desired effects more likely.

Internal Validity

Internal validity is the ability to attribute an effect to a given cause—the primary purpose of an experimental study. Single-subject experiments are frequently very strong in terms of internal validity (McCormick, 1990). The researchers typically employ a number of control procedures that contribute to the internal validity of their studies, including the systematic initiation and withdrawal of treatments, the use of subjects as their own controls, and the ongoing measurement of effects over time. Nevertheless, there exist possibilities that causes other than the treatment contributed to the observed outcome.

Qualitative data can aid literacy researchers in identifying and controlling potentially interfering or confounding variables and, therefore, increase internal validity. Such methods include the collection of detailed, descriptive information about the participants through individual interviews, and specific field notes documenting circumstances under which the intervention was implemented. These methods provide information about conditions outside the treatment in which subjects have been involved that could affect the target outcome of intervention. For example, observations tracing student engagement within various contexts (such as other school settings or home) might add to researchers' ability to explain their findings and entertain alternative explanations for observed effects. These data could assist researchers in gathering additional evidence related to their intervention claims, allowing them to more confidently address alternative explanations of their findings and strengthen the internal validity of their study.

External Validity

External validity is the ability to apply the results of a study to other subjects, settings, and times. Single-subject research is most often criticized with respect to this form of validity (McCormick, 1990; McReynolds & Kearns, 1983). Critics claim that results obtained from studies of only one subject or a few subjects cannot be generalized to larger groups of subjects.

The primary method that single-subject researchers use for dealing with issues of external validity is replication with different subjects, in different settings, or at different times. Although we recognize the value of replication across contexts, we believe that combining replication with other qualitative methods of data collection can provide the strongest evidence of external validity.

Although case-study research suffers from similar criticisms concerning generalizability, case-study designs tend to be strong in one aspect of external validity: ecological validity. This form of validity refers to the degree to which research findings represent the real world and are not limited to the potentially artificial conditions of a study.

One of the primary advantages of single-subject research is its emphasis on individuals' learning—finding out what works with a particular individual in a given context (McReynolds & Kearns, 1983). Qualitative information about the particular individual and learning context can provide details that can help researchers predict treatment effects in real-world situations (for example, when used by teachers with their students in classrooms; when used in contexts outside of school). For example, a study on reciprocal teaching might examine whether some students' success in the program reflected a more general ability to lead peers. In-depth interviews or observation data on students' functions in other group contexts before, during, and after the intervention could provide this information.

We believe that the incorporation into single-subject studies of more descriptive data about the specific contexts can provide the kind of evidence needed for researchers to be confident of the conditions under which the intervention is likely to have the most positive effect. It can help individuals who are likely to apply the results of the study (teachers, for example) make judgments about the ease with which the research intervention could be successfully implemented within their specific context, while providing additional direction in terms of factors crucial to achieving desired and transferable effects. See Palincsar and Brown (1984) for an example of a carefully reasoned combination design.

Summary and Conclusions

In addition to providing support for the criteria for judging the quality of intervention studies, using case-study methods within single-subject experimental designs helps raise and address associated research questions, such as how and why an effect may have occurred. Further, incorporating case-study questions and methods that address the learning context from more than one perspective may guide the development of the overall research line. Selecting and combining research methods from alternative paradigms can lead to logical, coherent single-subject designs that ultimately strengthen and enhance the value of resulting data.

Although single-subject and case-study approaches may be described as opposing, we believe that the two traditions can be mutually beneficial if combined with careful consideration of relevant theoretical issues raised by the paradigm debate. Research in education is particularly challenging due to the need to use the results to affect changes across a variety of educational settings. We must take seriously our responsibilities as researchers to provide thorough descriptions of a study's events, while making clear when causation may be inferred. We believe that an openness to combining methodologies in meaningful ways is a step in that direction.

References

Cherryholmes, C.H. (1992). Notes on pragmatism and scientific realism. *Educational Researcher, 21*(6), 13–17.

Clay, M. (1979). *The early detection of reading difficulties.* Portsmouth, NH: Heinemann.

Eisner, E.W. (1991). *The enlightened eye: Qualitative inquiry and the enhancement of educational practice.* New York: Macmillan.

Erickson, F. (1986). Qualitative methods in research on teaching. In M.C. Wittrock (Ed.), *Handbook of research on teaching* (3rd ed., pp. 119–161). New York: Macmillan.

Gage, N.L. (1989). The paradigm wars and their aftermath. *Educational Researcher, 18*(7), 4–10.

Garrison, J.W. (1986). Some principles of postpositivist philosophy of science. *Educational Researcher, 15*(9), 12–18.

Geller, E.S. (1991). Where's the validity in social validity? *Journal of Applied Behavior Analysis, 24*(2), 179-184.

Goatley, V.J., Brock, C.H., & Raphael, T.E. (1993, February). *Diverse learners participating in regular education "book clubs."* Paper presented at the annual meeting of the University of Pennsylvania Ethnography Forum, Philadelphia, PA.

Hersh, S. (1990). *Research on teaching: A comparison between qualitative strategies and behavior analysis strategies.* Paper presented at the annual meeting of the Association Behavior Analysts, Nashville, TN.

Howe, K.R. (1985). Two dogmas of educational research. *Educational Researcher, 14*(8), 10–18.

Howe, K.R., & Eisenhart, M. (1990). Standards for qualitative (and quantitative) research: A prolegomenon. *Educational Researcher, 19*(4), 2–9.

Kuhn, T.S. (1962). *The structure of scientific revolutions* (2nd. ed.). Chicago, IL: University of Chicago Press.

McCormick, S. (1990). A case for the use of single-subject methodology in reading research. *Journal of Research in Reading, 13*(1), 69–81.

McReynolds, L.V., & Kearns, K.P. (1983). *Single-subject experimental designs in communicative disorders.* Austin, TX: PRO-ED.

Miles, M.B., & Huberman, A.M. (1984). Drawing valid meaning from qualitative data: Toward a shared craft. *Educational Researcher, 13*(5), 20–30.

Miller, S.I., & Fredericks, M. (1991). Postpositivistic assumptions and educational research: Another view. *Educational Researcher, 20*(4), 2–8.

Mudre, L.H., & McCormick, S. (1989). Effects of meaning-focused cues on underachieving readers' context use, self-corrections, and literal comprehension. *Reading Research Quarterly*, *24*(1), 89–113.

Palincsar, A.S., & Brown, A.L. (1984). Reciprocal teaching of comprehension-fostering and comprehension-monitoring activities. *Cognition & Instruction*, *1*, 117–175.

Phillips, D.C. (1983). After the wake: Postpositivistic educational thought. *Educational Researcher*, *12*(5), 4–12.

Rist, R.C. (1977). On the relations among educational research paradigms: From disdain to détente. *Anthropology & Education*, *8*(2), 42–49.

Rist, R.C. (1980). Blitzkrieg ethnography: On the transformation of a method into a movement. *Educational Researcher*, *9*(2), 8–10.

Rizo, F.M. (1991). The controversy about quantification in social research: An extension of Gage's "historical sketch." *Educational Research*, *20*(9), 9–12.

Schwartz, I.S., & Baer, D.M. (1991). Social validity assessments: Is current practice state of the art? *Journal of Applied Behavior Analysis*, *24*, 189–204.

Van Houten, R. (1979). Social validation: The evolution of standards of competency for target behaviors. *Journal of Applied Behavior Analysis*, *12*, 581–591.

Winett, R.A., Moore, J.F., & Anderson, E.S. (1991). Extending the concept of social validity: Behavior analysis for disease prevention and health promotion. *Journal of Applied Behavior Analysis*, *24*, 215–230.

Wolf, M.M. (1978). Social validity: The case for subjective measurement or how applied behavior analysis is finding its heart. *Journal of Applied Behavior Analysis*, *11*, 203–214.

CHAPTER 7

Teachers Using Single-Subject Designs in the Classroom

Judith A. Braithwaite

Historical documentation of the concept of teachers as researchers can be found as early as the late 1800s. Then and in the early 1900s, authorities can cite incidents where teachers were involved in gathering data, drawing conclusions, and reporting results. Although these activities were not identified as research and were primitive compared to today's investigative standards, they were characteristic of what has become known as educational research (Olson, 1990).

Throughout its history, the concept of teachers as researchers has been controversial. However, in recent years, there have been more calls for increased connection between theory and practice, and a call for teachers to become more involved as research consumers and researchers (Hopkins, 1985).

Signs that teacher-research has become a valid, acceptable professional practice are evident:

1. Observations and descriptive research are now seen as valid forms of data collection (Casanova, 1989).

2. Teachers and researchers are working together in classrooms in a reciprocal rather than hierarchical relationship (Casanova, 1989).

3. Reflective thinking is seen as an important element of effective teaching, a concept inherent to research (Posner, 1989; Schön, 1983).

4. Teachers are involved in site-based management, in decision making that opens the door for teachers to be consumers as well as participants in research.

5. Programs using peer evaluation and mentoring in the assessment of teaching performance are promoting opportunities for teacher research (Geiger, 1990).

6. Components of teacher research are part of the assessment tools employed for evaluating teaching performance (National Board for Professional Teaching Standards, 1991).

7. Calls for proposals from federal and state agencies may include teacher research (*Education Grants Alert*, 1993).

In addition to these movements, the rationale for teachers to be researchers seems simple and to the point for four reasons. First, classrooms—the students' learning environment—are where the action, questions, and concerns are most likely to arise. For example, the single-subject alternating-treatments design (see Chapter 4) used in a study discussed later in this chapter, grew out of a teacher's concern about the inconsistency between end-of-level test results and a student's actual performance with authentic reading materials. In this teacher's school district, the monitoring of students' progress in reading was reported to administrators via basal reader tests, but the tests did not appear to represent the students' reading progress in the classroom. By collecting actual data about students' contrasting reading responses on the tests versus those on authentic reading tasks, the teacher was able to substantiate this point.

Second, teachers have access to large amounts of data in the form of observations and permanent products. These can be organized in a meaningful way to answer educational questions. Farr and Carey (1986), for example, discuss a need for more research that will describe and analyze the potential of informal reading assessment. The classroom teacher has opportunities to make an impact on this area where research is greatly needed.

Third, teachers have extended contact with students, which can add insight to research findings. For example, in analyzing the results of one study on the use of maze sentences in assessment, the teacher conducting the research was able to incorporate evidence from numerous occasions across time. This evidence indicated that students in the study had experienced difficulty with this type of modified cloze test in the past. Taking this information into account provided more depth to the discussion of the findings and is an example of the qualitative data that Bisesi and Raphael (Chapter 6 of this volume) recommend collecting.

Fourth, teachers need to be knowledgeable consumers of research. Personal involvement in data collection promotes awareness of the potential and limitations of research, which, in turn, can help teachers to be effective decision makers (McCormick, 1987). In today's world of educational accountability, instructional and assessment tools must be based on accurate research findings that are the result of sound studies conducted by others (Hopkins, 1985) and on data collected in the classroom.

Once teachers become involved with classroom research, its value becomes apparent to them through several benefits. A major benefit is that the process of research brings them into contact with professional literature and provides opportunities for thoughtful conversations about important topics with other educators. These acts alone broaden their knowledge base, bringing greater self-confidence in their teaching and decision-making abilities.

A second benefit is that classroom research can be a vehicle for greater collegiality and collaboration among teachers, administrators, and other educators. Involving school community members as observers to verify independent and dependent variables or as partners in the development and implementation of a study promotes support and communication that continues to grow beyond the initial research project. For example, at one school, teachers have formed two inquiry groups whose members included κ–5 teachers, an administrator, and a college professor who supports teacher research. These groups meet on a regular basis to discuss issues related to everyday teaching as well as plans of action to follow through on school-based research results (Kieffer, 1994).

A third benefit is that teacher research provides validation of theories and enhanced teaching practices. Monahan (1987), for instance, found that the classroom research in which she and other teachers participated led to the verification of the value of an instructional procedure for their classroom settings. The success of the strategy was communicated to others— parents, students, and administrators. As a result, teachers assumed ownership of and enhanced their teaching practices, and students became the beneficiaries as their achievement improved.

Although many benefits to teacher-researchers could be recounted, the final one to be shared reflects an ancient Chinese proverb: "Tell me—I forget; show me—I remember; involve me—I understand." Through active participation in classroom research, teachers better understand themselves as professionals, their students as learners, and the relationship between educational theory and practice. This knowledge and understanding leads to empowerment, which enables teaching professionals to be reflective, effective change agents for the betterment of all students.

A Teacher's Use of Single-Subject Experimental Research Designs

Measurement, analysis, and reflective thinking promote successful teaching and student achievement. Single-subject experimental designs provide classroom teachers with a viable research strategy for engaging in these processes. Lovitt (1977), for example, found that single-subject designs allowed teachers not only to evaluate the effectiveness of teaching strategies by measuring students' progress but also to communicate students' progress accurately to others. Conducting single-subject research also helps teachers develop professionally by gathering data, reflecting on the products of their efforts, refining the methods employed, and learning the true meaning of individual differences.

The following sections describe three examples of single-subject experimental research projects conducted by the author in a large, metropolitan school district. Each sample illustrates a different design: an A-B-A design, a multiple-baseline design, and an alternating-treatments design (see Chapters 2, 3, and 4 of this volume for in-depth descriptions of these designs). In each research project, the students were members of a regular classroom who were identified as reading disabled; they came from low socioeconomic backgrounds, based on federal guidelines that determine eligibility for free and reduced-cost school meals. The experimenter was a teacher who sought reliable data for the purposes of solving problems she observed in the regular classroom setting.

The examples in the following sections, though summarized versions of typical research reports, provide a fair degree of detail to demonstrate what teachers can do in single-subject data collection and to provide a model for others.

A-B-A Design

In the following example, the direct measurement of permanent products (see Chapter 1) was translated into numerical terms of response frequencies, or the number of times a response occurs in some time period (Cooper, 1981). This study was conducted to determine if computer use during journal-writing sessions would increase the amount of text written in a journal by a student who had difficulty expressing himself in longhand during daily journal-writing sessions.

Method. Darwin was a fourth grade African American male whose reading level was approximately second grade. All writing sessions occurred in a regular classroom with 23 other fourth grade students. The dependent variable was the numbers of words Darwin wrote when composing text during journal-writing sessions. The independent variable was his use of the classroom computer to write his journal entries.

Journal writing sessions were held every school day from 9:00 to 9:30 a.m. for 15 days. To evaluate the continued effect of computer use on Darwin's journal writing, additional assessments (often called *postchecks*) were conducted at 1-, 3-, and 5-week intervals following the study. Darwin used a notebook for longhand journal entries and a word-processing program with a spell-checker for computer journal sessions. Sessions began in January and adhered to previous guidelines followed by the students for journal-writing periods: the writing topic was chosen by the students, a quiet working atmosphere was encouraged to permit thoughtful reflection, and volunteers shared journal entries with the class after each session.

At the end of each journal-writing session, Darwin counted the words entered in his journal and recorded the number on a small graph prepared by the teacher. Prior to each writing session, the teacher challenged Darwin to increase the number of words he wrote. The teacher-researcher and school principal acted as independent scorers to determine the reliability of Darwin's count of the number of words written. Each scorer randomly selected the sessions he or she would evaluate.

Results and discussion. Interscorer agreement was computed for 10 of 18 journal-writing sessions (including 3 during the maintenance period), or 56 percent of the total number of sessions.

Figure 7.1 shows the length of the text Darwin produced during the journal-writing sessions. Following a low rate of words produced during baseline 1, when he tried to write his journal entries in longhand, Darwin produced longer text under the computer-use intervention. Darwin's writing behavior returned to its low rate during baseline 2, when he wrote in longhand again, but increased to its highest level during the maintenance (postcheck) phase in which computer use was again in effect.

From the graph, it is evident that when Darwin used the computer during journal-writing sessions, the length of his texts increased. The postchecks during the maintenance assessments indicate that continued use of the computer increased his production. An analysis of entries written by Darwin revealed two additional benefits of computer use: increased use of descriptive words and more story-like text.

Darwin participated in this study both as a subject and a researcher. When asked why he thought the length of his journal entries increased during the computer-use phase, he immediately responded, "I don't have to worry about messing up my paper...the computer fixes it," "My fingers don't get cramped," and "There's a speller brain...my words look good."

To strengthen the conclusion as to the controlling forces of the intervention, the teacher replicated the study with five other students who had similar journal-writing characteristics.

Multiple-Baseline Design

Since some behaviors should not (or cannot) be reversed as was done in the previous example (see Yaden, Chapter 2, and Kucera and Axelrod, Chapter 3), the teacher employed a multiple-baseline design (which does not require reversal of the responses) to examine the effects of partner-

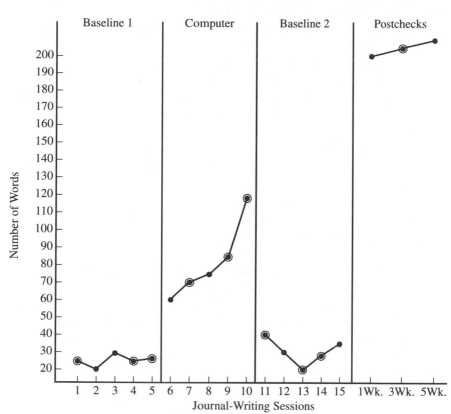

Figure 7.1
Number of Words Written by Darwin During Journal-Writing Sessions

Note: Points with circles around them indicate interobserver data.

reading. Specifically, this teacher wanted to determine if partner-reading might increase students' comprehension of connected reading material over their preintervention levels when they read alone.

Method. The subjects were six fifth grade students whose average reading level was approximately 4.0. All activities occurred in a regular classroom with 22 other fifth graders.

The dependent variable was the number of correct responses to comprehension questions. The independent variable was a partner-reading strategy. A series of 30 short stories was used as connected-text reading material. Following each story, students responded to seven questions to check their comprehension of text. During partner-reading, the target students were to take turns reading paragraphs and asking questions until they had completed the reading selection. Prior to the study, the students had completed a series of lessons on how to ask good questions using guidelines specified by Bloom's (1956) taxonomy.

All 28 students in the class individually read, responded to questions, and recorded their scores. During the baseline condition, students read alone. During intervention the six targeted students were randomly placed in pairs. During baseline and intervention, each student in a targeted pair answered questions independently after reading the story. Scores of each pair were averaged since each member of a pair, in effect, influenced the other's question-answering behavior.

The intervention strategy was initially applied to only one pair following baseline (see Figure 7.2), while the other two pairs continued in baseline status (see Chapter 3 for the rationale for these procedures). After correct responses increased for the first pair, then partner-reading was introduced to Group 2; when correct responses increased for Group 2, partner-reading was applied with Group 3.

Reading sessions were held on consecutive school days for a total of 30 sessions. Data collection began the last week of October. Two fifth grade teachers randomly selected 16 (or 53 percent) of the sessions for which they acted as independent scorers. Interscorer agreement averaged 98.6 percent.

Results and discussion. Figure 7.2 shows the students' average number of correct responses to comprehension questions following their reading of connected text during the baseline condition (reading alone) and during the intervention (using the partner-reading strategy). Analysis of the graph shows that the partner-reading strategy had a positive effect on students' average number of correct responses. Main-idea questions were the ones most frequently missed. Difficulty with this question type may account for the pairs' inability to reach or maintain an average of seven correct responses.

Alternating-Treatments Design

Many basal programs provide tests at the end of each unit of stories, often referred to as end-of-level tests. Results on these tests are frequently used to move students forward in the reading program or keep them back, or to communicate the status of a specific reading program to district administrators. The teacher, in this particular example, observed inconsistencies between the results on the end-of-level tests and students' actual performance in classroom reading. To examine this issue, she used the alternating-treatments design (see Chapter 4) to collect data about these contrasting behaviors as they related specifically to word recognition. She chose the alternating-treatments design because with it the effects of two or more discrete conditions on student performance can be compared quick-

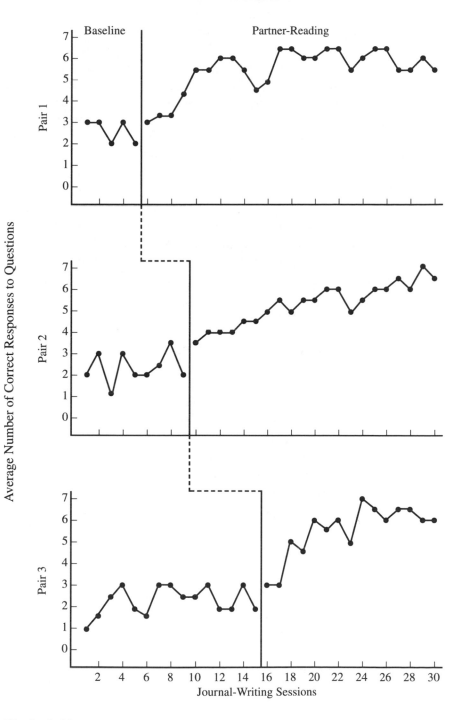

Figure 7.2
Average Number of Correct Responses to Comprehension Questions by Three Pairs of Students

ly without an initial baseline. In addition, conditions are randomly assigned to sessions to minimize sequence effect, which can threaten validity (Cooper, 1981).

Experimental control is demonstrated in the alternating-treatments design through prediction, verification, and replication. In this design, each successive data point plotted for a specific condition serves as (1) a reference point for the prediction of future levels of performance under that condition; (2) verification of prior predictions of behavior under that condition; and (3) a replication of differential effects produced by the other conditions that are part of the experiment (Cooper, Heron, & Heward, 1987).

Method. The teacher selected three commonly used word-recognition tests and one prose-passage test (similar to an authentic reading task) as the conditions of the alternating treatments design. Two of the tests, teacher-pronounced tests and maze-sentence tests, are frequently used as end-of-level tests. The teacher-pronounced test procedures require the students to circle one of three words based on the test administrator's pronunciation of the target word. The maze-sentence test, sometimes called a modified cloze test, directs students to independently read a sentence and select one of three words printed under a blank space:

The dog has _____ legs.
      fit four for

The third word-recognition test selected, the word-card test, is often referred to as a flashcard assessment. The word-card test is used to evaluate students' word recognition in isolation. Students are asked to view one word at a time, responding to each within a specified time period.

The prose-passage test represented an authentic reading condition. Using evaluation procedures similar to a reading miscue analysis, students read a story containing words that were also on the teacher-pronounced tests, maze-sentence tests, and word-card tests. To complete the assessment, a comprehension check was included that asked students to retell what they read.

The subjects of this study were 6 second grade students—5 boys and 1 girl ranging in age from 7 to 8 years old—all of whom were reading from 1 year to 2.7 years below grade level. One child was Caucasian; five were African American. The data-collection sites were a classroom containing 25 additional second graders and the hall directly outside the classroom. All data were collected by the teacher during regular school hours.

The dependent variables measured were the students' correct responses to word-recognition tasks on the teacher-pronounced tests, maze-sentences tests, word-card tests, and prose-passage tests. A comparison was made of the students' responses to the same words tested in the other three tests when the student was reading the prose-passage tests under an independent reading condition.

In all cases, a correct response was defined as 100 percent agreement between the text word and the students' pronunciation or selection. For the words on the other three tests to be a predictor of a student's response to that word in the connected text of the prose-passage test, there had to be a match in response correctness. For example, if a student missed "rug" on the teacher-pronounced test, then he or she also had to miss it on the prose-passage test. If a student correctly responded to the word "up" on the teacher-pronounced test, then "up" also had to be correct on the prose-passage test.

In this study, the type of test administration was the independent variable. To help control this variable, a script for each test type was prepared and used by the teacher to administer each test.

Test sessions were held twice a day, once in the morning and once in the afternoon, for a total of 32 sessions in 16 days. Each test was administered to each student 8 times. All sessions were recorded on audiotape and a stopwatch was used to ensure accuracy of allotted time for students' responses.

The teacher-pronounced tests and maze-sentences tests were group "paper and pencil" tests and were administered by the teacher to the six target students in the classroom. The word-card tests and prose-passage tests were administered to individual students in the hall just outside the classroom door.

Independent scorers were used to determine reliability of test scores (dependent variables), and observers assessed the degree of correctness of test administration using the teacher's prepared test scripts and audiotape recordings to evaluate the integrity of the independent variable (see Chapter 1 of this volume). These other staff members who served as scorers and observers were trained for these tasks after school on three occasions. Interscorer agreement was computed for 132 of the 192 samples (69 percent of the total test samples administered). Interobserver agreement was computed for 54 of the 192 samples (28 percent).

Results and discussion. Figure 7.3 illustrates individual student performance on all test types. Table 7.1 shows that 70.2 percent of the time the word-card tests predicted performance on the prose-passage tests. Teacher-pronounced tests were predictors 59 percent of the time, while maze-sentences were predictors 58.1 percent of the time. Percentage of prediction accuracy of the word-card tests for reading accuracy on prose passages was greatest for all students except Tim.

Example of analysis: Teacher-pronounced tests. Since the purpose of this chapter is to demonstrate how teacher researchers can use single-

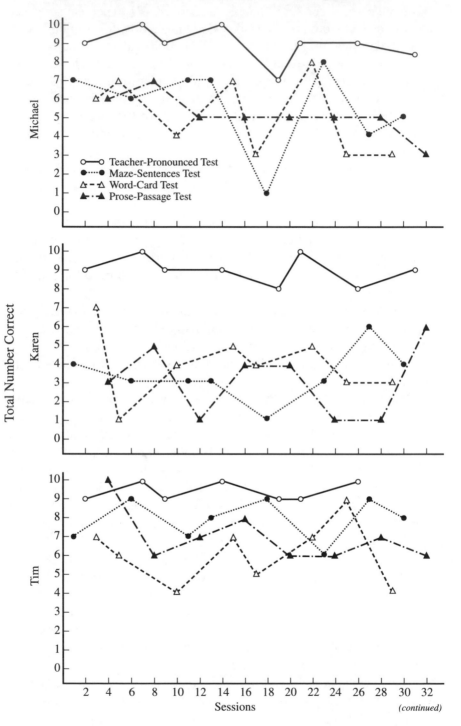

Figure 7.3
Individual Student's Raw Scores on Word-Recognition Tests

○—○ Teacher-Pronounced Test
●·····● Maze-Sentences Test
△– –△ Word-Card Test
▲·–·▲ Prose-Passage Test

Michael

Karen

Total Number Correct

Tim

Sessions

(continued)

Figure 7.3
Individual Student's Raw Scores on Word-Recognition Tests (cont'd.)

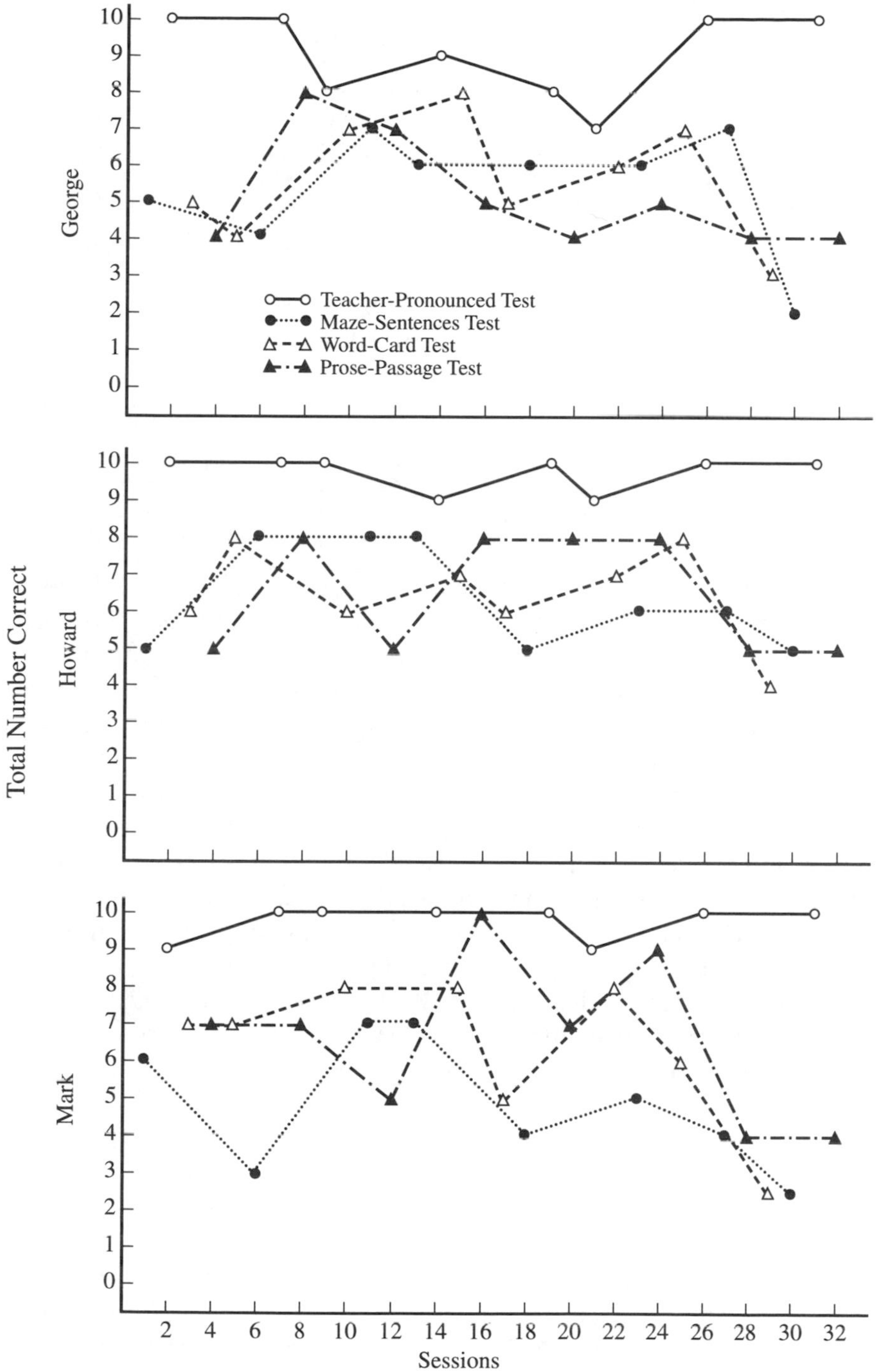

○—○ Teacher-Pronounced Test
●····● Maze-Sentences Test
△--△ Word-Card Test
▲-·-▲ Prose-Passage Test

Table 7.1
Percentage of Time Teacher-Pronounced (T-P), Maze-Sentences (M-S), and Word-Card (W-C) Tests Predicted Performance on the Prose-Passage Tests

Student	Test Type		
	T-P	M-S	W-C
Clarence	56.3	55	65
Karl	68.8	52.5	76.2
Kenyana	33.8	60	66.3
Kerry	67.5	62.5	78.8
Marcus	55	55	72.5
Tommy	72.5	63.8	62.5
Group Mean	59	58.1	70.2

subject experimental designs to analyze information obtained in classrooms (and not to provide all the details of this specific study), an analysis of data from only one of the test types will be given here. The alternating-treatments design provides a graphic presentation that is easy to analyze. When this analysis was combined with an evaluation of students' specific responses, the teacher could easily determine which, if any, test types were effective predictors of a student's reading ability in connected materials. A visual analysis of the data, displayed graphically in Figure 7.3, revealed that data points for the teacher-pronounced tests and prose-passage tests were characterized by minimum overlap. Overlap occurred only once each for George, Mark, and Tim. This evidence shows there is little relationship between the teacher-pronounced tests and prose-passage tests. The degree of differential effect produced by the two test types ranged from 2.5 words for Tim to Karen's mean difference of 5.9 words. The group mean difference between the two test types, as can be determined from the graphs in Figure 7.3, was 3.7 words, an educationally significant difference when considering that each test only contained 10 items (see Chapter 4, this volume). On average, students made correct selections for 4 of the 10 words when they were pronounced by the teacher—yet, they could not recognize them in connected-text reading situations. The trend of the data was consistent across both test types, which supports the reliability of the results.

The graphic analysis of raw scores supports the findings of Ekwall (1973) and others which state that results obtained in a situation that is not analogous to actual reading can be misleading. In this case it was easier for the students to choose one word pronounced by the teacher from a choice of three on the teacher-pronounced tests than it was to read the same word orally in connected reading.

Table 7.1 shows that for the total group, the teacher-pronounced test only predicted performance on the prose-passage test 59 percent of the time. The highest percentage of prediction was for Tim, whose teacher-pronounced-test scores predicted his performance on the prose-passage tests 72.5 percent of the time. Karen had the lowest percentage of prediction at 33.8 percent. For George and Michael and for the group as a whole, the teacher-pronounced test was equal to the maze-sentences test as a predictor of prose reading performance. For Mark and Howard, the teacher-pronounced test was the second best predictor. However, the mean percentage of prediction (59 percent) for all students was too low for the teacher to recommend this test as a diagnostic tool for promoting students to the next reading level or to predict words students would read correctly or incorrectly during oral reading of authentic prose materials.

When test developers of basal reader programs provide raw-score criterion as a level of mastery on a test, they are indicating that raw scores are predictors of a student's prose reading skill—that is, his or her skill in reading connected, authentic texts. The raw-score criterion (mastery level) sometimes used for teacher-pronounced tests in basal reader programs is approximately 8 out of 10 items correct. Using this criterion and the raw scores from the teacher-pronounced tests in the study, all 6 students reached mastery on all test sessions except for two. (In these latter two sessions George and Michael each scored 7 out of 10 correct.) These raw scores could lead to the assumption that the students could read the same words in an actual reading situation. Yet, when the students' scores from the teacher-pronounced tests are examined in relationship to their scores on the prose-passage tests, a different conclusion becomes apparent.

Some conclusions from this study are the following:

1. Raw scores on basal reader end-of-level-tests are not effective measures for predicting these students' performance with connected reading materials.

2. Teacher-pronounced tests are not effective in predicting a student's performance on prose passages.

3. Although graphic analysis shows the maze-sentences test could be used as a predictor of students' connected reading skills, an evaluation of specific words shows it is not the most effective predictor for all students.

4. For the total group, the word-card tests in which students were required to pronounce words in isolation are the best predictors of students' performances in connected reading materials.

Commentary

The sample studies shared in this chapter demonstrate that teacher-researchers using single-subject designs can help meet challenges in reading assessment and instruction. For example, the alternating-treatments study just described extends Ekwall's (1976) study on teacher-pronounced tests, furthers the findings of Flood and Lapp (1987) on the relationship of end-of-level testing and basal reading, and broadens Goodman's (1965) study of primary-level readers. More important, however, the studies described through the previous section had an immediate impact on the instructional procedures being used in the classroom. Through data collection and analysis, teachers are able to make research-based decisions that enhance the learning environment for students. For example, by simply introducing and measuring the effect computer use had on students' journal writing, one teacher helped students produce writing that better reflected their age and ability. In addition, this provided a strong rationale for increased access to classroom computers and open-ended writing time.

A teacher's ability to conduct single-subject experimental research develops over time. Transition into a more data-based instructional program may require several months or more for most teachers. To encourage teacher-researchers to conduct single-subject research and data-based instructional programs, Cooper (1981) offers the following suggestions. First, the teacher should begin with measuring and graphing one or two conditions (or behaviors) for one student, then gradually extend these same measures to other students. For example, in one third grade class, four students were experiencing difficulty in acquiring automaticity in reading irregular words. The teacher chose one of the four students for an intervention strategy to increase automatic recognition, measuring and graphing baseline and intervention data. Later, the same intervention strategy was introduced to the other students with the same measures and graphing employed.

Second, teachers should record students' responses for the shortest period of time possible (making sure it is sufficient to provide a sample of the condition). The suggested rule is that the measurement period can be short if the behavior occurs at a high rate, but all occurrences should be measured if they happen only once or twice per day. For example, if the teacher is recording the number of times a student self-corrects while reading connected material across subject areas in a self-contained classroom, then a two-minute sampling during each of the student's daily readings would be sufficient since the student has many opportunities to respond. However, if the teacher is measuring the total number of words a student writes during daily 20-minute journal-writing times, this should be recorded each day, since the student has only one opportunity to respond.

Third, teachers can use teacher aides, volunteers, and students to help measure and graph conditions. The minimal training required to prepare these valuable resource persons is an investment worth making. Students especially benefit from participating as their own recorders. Because this focuses students on their behavior, it can serve as motivation to change. In addition, it can also enhance students' opportunities for problem solving and reflective thinking about themselves as learners. In the study employing the A-B-A design discussed earlier, for example, Darwin used information from the graphing of his journal-writing behavior to make collaborative decisions with his teacher about how he might improve his writing.

Finally, Cooper (1981) suggests that teachers collaborate with university teachers, administrators, and peers skilled in measurement and graphing. This kind of support is especially important during the initial stages because it provides opportunities for teachers to discuss appropriate techniques and strategies, increase their knowledge base on graphic analysis and alternative techniques for measuring and graphing, and receive encouragement during times of frustration. Teachers' contact with these resource persons promotes collegiality, collaborative planning, and general networking, all vital to the professional characteristics of effective teaching.

In addition, teachers should remember that during the transitional period they will experience some trial and error as they experiment with different techniques. Patience with themselves and reflective thinking about the process are crucial to success. For example, a teacher may decide to record students' responses during a 20-minute reading period. After 3 days, the teacher realizes that it is impossible to record 5 students' responses for a full 20 minutes and changes to 2-minute samplings from each student during reading time.

It is important for teachers to remember that one of the major advantages to single-subject experimental research is that graphs can be analyzed each day so that changes in interventions can be made immediately. During one study of an intervention strategy used to increase students' understanding of the concept of main ideas, for example, the teacher graphed the number of correct responses that students had recorded on audiotape. An analysis of the graphs showed that students were not improving. The teacher decided to make a change in the intervention strategy, which resulted in students' increased understanding of main ideas. The flexibility of single-subject research allows such changes to be made.

The current school-restructuring movement in the United States and elsewhere brings with it an opportunity for teachers to produce research that can become a valid, reliable form of investigation into educational issues at a local level. One way teachers can begin this journey toward truly reflective, effective teaching is through the use of single-subject experimental research in their own classrooms.

References

Bloom, B. (1956). *Taxonomy of educational objectives*. White Plains, NY: Longman.

Casanova, U. (1989). Research and practice: We can integrate them. *NEA Today*, 7(6), 44–49.

Cooper, J.O. (1981). *Measuring behavior* (2nd ed.). Columbus, OH: Merrill.

Cooper, J.O., Heron, T.E., & Heward, W.L. (1987). *Applied behavior analysis*. Columbus, OH: Merrill.

Education grants alert. (1993). Alexandria, VA: Capitol.

Ekwall, E.E. (1973). *An analysis of children's test scores when tested with individually administered diagnostic tests and when tested with group administered diagnostic tests* (Final Research Report). El Paso, TX: University of Texas, University Research Institute.

Farr, R., & Carey, R.F. (1986). *Reading: What can be measured?* (2nd ed.). Newark, DE: International Reading Association.

Flood, J., & Lapp, D. (1987). Types of writing in basal readers and assessment tests: An imperfect match. *The Reading Teacher*, 40, 880–883.

Geiger, K. (1990, June). *Keynote address*. Paper presented at the meeting of the National Education Association, Kansas City, KS.

Goodman, K.S. (1965). A linguistic study of cues and miscues in reading. *Elementary English*, 42, 639–643.

Hopkins, D. (1985). *A teacher's guide to classroom research*. Philadelphia, PA: Open University Press.

Kieffer, J.C. (1994). Bringing a new order to things. In M. Dalheim (Ed.), *School-based change*. Washington, DC: National Education Association.

Lovitt, T.C. (1977). *In spite of my resistance: I've learned from children*. Columbus, OH: Merrill.

McCormick, S. (1987). *Remedial and clinical reading instruction*. Columbus, OH: Merrill.

Monahan, J. (1987). Changing content instruction through action research. *Journal of Reading*, 30, 676–678.

National Board for Professional Teaching Standards. (1991). *Initial policies and perspectives of the National Board of Professional Teaching Standards* (2nd ed.). Detroit, MI: Author.

Olson, M.W. (1990). The teacher as researcher: A historical perspective. In M.W. Olson (Ed.), *Opening the doors to classroom research*. Newark, DE: International Reading Association.

Posner, G.J. (1989). *Field experience: Methods of reflective teaching* (2nd ed.). White Plains, NY: Longman.

Schön, D.A. (1983). *Educating the reflective practitioner*. San Francisco, CA: Jossey-Bass.

CHAPTER 8

Important Issues Related to Single-Subject Experimental Research

Annemarie Sullivan Palincsar
Andrea DeBruin Parecki

This is an exciting time to be engaged in research. The positivist tradition, which suggests that research must be limited to those questions that can be pursued through prescribed methods, has yielded to a postpositivist understanding of science in which no single method is seen as correct; rather the choice of methodology must be guided by the principle of finding the approach most responsive to the particular question at hand, the method that will lead to a deeper and richer understanding of the question that has been posed. It is in this spirit that we have written this chapter. Our purpose is not to argue for or against the value of single-subject experimental research, but rather to provide some considerations for those who are entertaining the idea of using the designs discussed in this book. In particular, we wish to describe factors that enhance or impede the success with which researchers can use single-subject methodology to attain rich and robust answers to their questions.

Setting the Context: A Brief History of Research Methodology

In a systematic survey of experimental psychological journals, Danziger (1990) illustrates that in virtually all studies published up to World War I, the results were clearly attributed to individual experimental subjects. Even in cases where results were averaged across subjects, the responses of each individual were systematically reported. Furthermore, it was the pattern of individual responses, and not an aggregate of the responses, that formed the basis of the theoretical discussion. Danziger argues that to understand this tradition, one must understand the way in which psychological knowledge was defined. Reflecting the influence of Wilhelm Wundt, who is often regarded as the father of modern psychology, psychological knowledge was seen to pertain to the content of individual minds. However, this was not to suggest that observed phenomena were idiosyncratic to individuals, since it was believed that there is a universality in the underlying physiology of all normal human individuals. Furthermore, claims for generality were supported by repeating the experiment with a few individuals—in other words, with the use of multiple-subject, single-intervention designs. Finally, in the event that replications were not successful, relevant personal information or introspective evidence, such as previous experience or fluctuating attention, was used to account for the discrepant results (procedures similar to those suggested by Bisesi and Raphael in Chapter 6 of this volume).

Roughly between 1914 and 1936, a significant trend is detected in Danziger's (1990) content analysis. In studies reported in five of the most prominent journals of basic and applied experimental research, there was a significant decline in the use of the individual in favor of the use of group data. This trend was first observed in those journals devoted primarily to "applied" study, although journals of "basic" research soon followed suit. For example, while 43 percent of the studies reported in the *Journal of Experimental Psychology* during 1914–1936 reported individual data only and 38 percent reported group data only, by 1949–1951, 15 percent reported individual data and 83 percent reported group data. In general, the only areas of psychological research that continued in the Wundtian tradition were studies of sensation and perception, areas in which this tradition was first introduced. Danziger (1990) advances an interesting explanation regarding the "triumph of the aggregate" that attributes this shift to multiple occurrences, including the following:

1. The adherence to the notion that to make claims about individuals it was not necessary to subject them to experimentation but rather only to compare an individual's performance with that of others and then assign him or her a place in some aggregate of performance.

2. The introduction of research tools such as the questionnaire, with the concomitant development of social statistics.

3. The adoption of an approach that would be more likely to appeal to the public, offer social relevance, and hence advance general support for the young discipline of scientific psychology.

Hersen and Barlow (1976) suggest that the reemergence of interest in research focusing on the individual or the study of groups using time as a variable was in response to a number of methodological, practical, and ethical problems inherent in group research. First, there are the ethical issues involved in withholding treatment from a no-treatment control group. Second, there are the practical problems associated with attempts to collect data from large numbers of individuals. Third, when results are averaged across a number of individuals, the responses of individuals are obscured; in addition, in group designs the only type of variability considered is what occurs among individuals, not that which occurs within individuals. Finally, there are the difficulties associated with generalizing findings from group data that do not speak to individual responses. One solution to these difficulties is the use of single-subject designs in which the participants serve as their own controls. As described earlier in this volume, in such studies performance in one condition is then compared with performance in another condition, and the dependent measures that are used to assess performance are collected repeatedly, over time as well as across conditions. Both inter- as well as intraindividual replications are used as evidence that there is a functional relationship between the independent and dependent variables.

With these issues in mind, we will proceed to discuss a number of the dimensions that need to be considered before single-subject designs can be used effectively. Many of these issues have been addressed in other chapters of this book. This chapter will provide a summary of many of the earlier arguments by organizing this discussion using a traditional scheme developed by Campbell and Stanley (1963): achieving internal and external validity.

Achieving Internal Validity

The question of internal validity relates to the extent to which one is assured that the manipulation of independent variables is responsible for changes in the dependent variables (Campbell & Stanley, 1963). Although the issues that we will present are not isolated to this methodology, there are certain characteristics of single-subject designs that pose special problems for internal validity. In this section, we consider the roles that history, testing effects, instrumentation and observation, and multiple-intervention interference might play in the course of using single-subject designs. These threats to internal validity are summarized in Table 8.1.

History

History pertains to events that are extraneous to the independent variable but that occur concurrently and may evince change in the dependent

Table 8.1
Summary of Potential Threats to Internal Validity

Threat	Addressing the Threat
History	• Documentation of incidents • Judicious selection of time for introduction of intervention • Analysis of confounding influences • Judicious selection of design
Testing effects	• Use of minimally intrusive measures • Examination of data for reactive or fatigue effects
Instrumentation and observation	• Use of interrater reliability measures • Random assignment of measurement instruments • Screening for instrument variability
Multiple-intervention interference	• Counterbalancing order of interventions • Judicious selection of design

variable. History poses a particular problem in single-subject designs to the extent that these studies generally occur over time, rendering it more possible for intervening events to occur. Consider the complexities in the lives of the young mothers with whom Neuman and Gallagher (1994) conducted their study of the effects of coaching mothers in an array of interactive patterns designed to enhance the literacy-related activity and growth of their young children. During the three months that the study occurred, these families experienced job losses, loss of shelter, and entanglements with law-enforcement officials. The researchers took great care to document these incidents in the lives of their participants; in fact, their report assumes many of the characteristics of case study (see Chapter 6).

The problems associated with history raise the question of when to introduce the intervention. One might argue that the intervention be introduced at some random point in time; in fact, many techniques used to analyze time-series data assume randomness (Kratochwill, 1978). However, given the contexts in which we conduct literacy research, such randomness is difficult to attain. An alternative is to be guided by some rule suggesting that the intervention be introduced at the point that baseline data indicate stability or reliability. At the very least, the researcher should select an intervention point that is least likely to coincide with an extraneous event. Finally, the researcher must examine all possible historical influences and—to the extent possible—conduct an analysis of confounding influences.

History as a threat to internal validity is somewhat reduced in the case of multiple-baseline designs in which observations are collected on all replicated behaviors in all settings, or across all participants during all phases of the study (see Chapter 3). For example, in the study referred to above, Neuman and Gallagher (1994) employed a multiple-baseline-across-behaviors design, in which data were collected on the three instructional strategies (labeling, scaffolding, and contingent responsivity) targeted in the intervention. The intervention was then applied to each behavior in turn, while data continued to be collected across all three behaviors for the duration of the study. The targeted behavior and only the targeted behavior changed when the mothers were coached in the use of each of the three strategies, supporting the inference that the intervention was indeed responsible for the changes in the mothers' literacy activity.

Another example is a study by Palincsar and Brown (1984), employing a multiple-baseline-across-subjects design. Four groups of students were in the baseline condition concurrently. Data collected daily during baseline included written responses to comprehension assessments that were done from recall of the text. The intervention was staggered such that one group had four days of baseline, the second group had six days, and the remaining two groups had eight days of baseline. The intervention was introduced first to the group that showed the greatest stability on the assessments during baseline. The staggered baseline was particularly important in this case since the results of students' assessments were being charted and shared with the students on a periodic basis. The first feedback session coincided with the first day of instruction for the students in group 1. Had there not been three other groups who remained in baseline, it would not have been possible to determine if the students' responses—as measured by the comprehension assessments—were a function of the instructional intervention or of the fact that the students were being given feedback regarding their performance during baseline.

Testing

A second threat to internal validity is the effect of testing. In conventional group designs, confounding due to testing occurs when improved scores are due, in part, to the participants having taken a pretest. In single-subject designs, one is basically administering a series of pretests. There are, of course, several possible outcomes of such repeated testing. One is a reactive effect in which the measurement process itself is a cause of change. We observed this effect in a recent study (Palincsar, Brown, & Campione,

1993) in which first graders listened to short passages and responded to a series of questions, one of which asked them to apply the information in the text to a novel problem, a second of which asked them to identify the gist of the passage, and the remainder of which were more traditional comprehension questions. Five assessments were administered during baseline and another ten during the course of the intervention. Although only students in the intervention showed gains across the three question types, students who remained in baseline showed gains on the gist question, apparently simply as a function of repeatedly being asked to talk about the gist of the passage. A second testing effect occurs when baseline performance becomes depressed as a function of fatigue or changes in motivation.

Testing effects can be addressed by attending to the intrusiveness of the measure that is being administered. Reactive and fatigue effects are less likely when less intrusive measures are used (such as naturalistic observations). In addition, it is important to examine the data for the possibility of reactive or fatigue effects.

Instrumentation and Observation

Another possible threat to internal validity can occur as a function of unreliable or inconsistent measurement. For example, when data are being collected through observation, observer drift or bias may occur over time. This suggests the importance of a robust observational scheme that can be examined for interrater reliability.

Although they plague comprehension research generally, passage effects certainly can play havoc in single-subject designs. In their single-subject research examining the effects of reciprocal teaching to enhance comprehension, Palincsar and Brown have attempted to address this instrumentation issue in two ways. In their studies with junior high students, the passages used to assess changes in comprehension ability were administered at random. In the studies with young children where it was not possible to assign the comprehension assessments randomly since they were designed to correspond with the instructional passages (that is, the assessment passages featured the same biological principle that had been presented in the instructional passages), the full complement of assessment passages was administered to 20 or more students to screen for variability. Passages for which there appeared to be clear passage effects were replaced.

Multiple-Intervention Interference

Multiple-intervention interference occurs when there are two or more interventions within the same study and the effect of the second or any subsequent intervention is attributed to the intervention itself when, in fact, it may be due to some combination of the intervention and previous interventions. For example, in the Neuman and Gallagher study (1994), mothers' responses to instruction in scaffolding may have been a function of what the mothers had learned and retained during the previous phase of instruction when they were coached in labeling. It is possible to control for multiple-intervention interference by counterbalancing the order of the interventions; for example, one pair of mothers might have been coached first in labeling, while another was coached in scaffolding, and yet a third was coached in contingent responsiveness. However, in the case of the Neuman and Gallagher study, one might argue that the sequencing of the interventions provided a useful way of gradually increasing the demands on the mothers. In this case, individuals attempting to replicate the initial outcomes in this research would simply want to observe the same order of intervention.

Another approach to addressing this threat to internal validity is to employ an alternating-treatments design in which interventions are alternated randomly until one intervention proves to be more effective than the others (see Chapter 4). This design is particularly appropriate when the target behavior is one that can change quickly, there is little likelihood of carryover effects, and it is possible for the learner to readily distinguish among the interventions. Given the thrust of most contemporary literacy research, these criteria are not easily met; however, there are some examples of this design in the literature. Rosenberg et al. (1992) used an alternating-treatments design to compare the effects of three error-correction procedures on the oral reading of four students identified as learning disabled. The three procedures, which were implemented as students read orally, were (1) word supply, which involved the teacher supplying the correct word when the student made an error; (2) drill, in which the teacher supplied the word but also engaged the student in repeated practice identifying error words; and (3) phonic drill rehearsal, in which the same procedures were in place as in the drill condition, with the addition of practice in sounding out the error words. During the first 20 days of instruction, treatment alternated between procedures 1 and 2; during the second 20 days, treatment alternated between procedures 2 and 3. Procedure 1 was dropped from the intervention during phase 2 since it had not proven to be as effective as procedure 2 during phase one. The alternations were conducted on a randomized basis such that each of the two procedures (in each phase) was implemented a total of 10 times. The results, as determined by assessing accuracy identifying previous error words, as well as measures of fluency, indicated that when the drill procedure was in effect, students showed the greatest increments in performance.

Achieving External Validity

External validity asks the question of generalizability: To what populations, settings, treatment variables, and measurement variables can the effects be generalized? (Campbell & Stanley, 1963). External validity, or replicability, is perhaps the most contentious issue in discussions of single-subject designs, given the limited sample size and the fact that the participants in the research are seldom selected randomly. In fact, generalizing from data is problematic, regardless of methodology, as there are numerous variables that can potentially influence the extrapolation of data from one context to another. Clearly, a number of the threats to internal validity that were identified in the preceding section are also threats to external validity. For example, multiple-intervention interference would make it difficult to determine if results would generalize to a second setting in which only one intervention was in place. Similarly, the effects of history would also impede generalization. In this section we consider generalizing to different populations, settings, and measures, and suggest standards that can be useful to assessing claims regarding the generalizability of findings from single-subject research. Table 8.2 presents a summary of these standards.

Table 8.2
Useful Standards for Assessing Claims Regarding Generalizability

Generalizing to	Standards
different populations	Do the researchers provide complete descriptions of demographic factors, environment-subject interactions, and participant-selection criteria?
different settings (i.e., the intervention and conditions in place during the conduct of the research)	Do the researchers provide a complete description of factors influencing and context of baseline performances and the nature and procedures of intervention?
different measures	Do the researchers examine the repeated measures taken to make judgments of the reliability of the measures and identify evidence of floor or ceiling effects?
a theory	Do the researchers provide evidence that supports the reliability of a specific theory or contributes to the generalizability of that theory?

Characterizing the Participants

Extrapolation from the sample to a population constitutes the strongest argument for generalization (Firestone, 1993). The strength of the argument is, in large part, a function of the similarities between the participants in the original research and those individuals to whom one wishes to generalize. How does one provide precise and complete descriptions of the participants for the purpose of facilitating generalization decisions? Rosenberg et al. (1992) suggest that two types of variables be considered: (1) demographic factors such as age, ethnicity, sex, socioeconomic status, and regional location, which, generally speaking, are impervious to educational interventions; and (2) environment-subject interactions including achievement levels, grade levels, and educational histories (such as participation in remedial or special education services). In a thoughtful critique of participant descriptions in single-subject research, Wolery and Exell (1993) recommend that, in addition to these two categories of factors, researchers also describe the criteria used to include and exclude the participants. They suggest that these criteria are likely to be more precise than the status variables traditionally used to describe the participants, and that they provide a better basis for making qualified statements about the effects of independent variables.

An excellent example of the inclusion of these three categories of information regarding participants is reported by Mudre and McCormick (1989) in their study of the use of meaning-focused cues on the reading activity and comprehension of underachieving students (this study is also described in Chapter 6). In addition to the standard demographic factors, they report the sequence of steps used in the selection process. Finally, they also identify not only which children were receiving remedial instruction, but they also describe the nature and focus of all language and literacy instruction in which the children were participating. By characterizing the emphases of instruction, the researchers allow the reader to consider how the intervention might be interacting with both the instructional histories and the instruction the children were receiving.

Characterizing the Setting

In this context we are using "setting" to refer to the intervention—that is, the subject of study as well as the conditions in place while the intervention is implemented and evaluated. One obvious way to address external validity is by providing a careful, thorough, and useful description of the intervention itself. Of course, this standard applies to the study of any intervention, regardless of the design used to determine its efficacy.

As researchers and teachers in the field of literacy move further away from interventions that are carefully controlled and scripted, characterizing the intervention becomes a more important issue. There are various models in the literature for doing so. One model is simply to present in the procedures section the complete set of directions observed by those involved in the intervention. This model is illustrated in the report of self-instructional strategy training conducted by Graham and Harris (1989) who used a multiple-baseline-across-subjects design to determine the effectiveness of teaching composition strategies. Another is to include dialogue illustrating the nature of the intervention, an approach used by Palincsar, Brown, and Campione (1993) in their investigation of reciprocal teaching dialogues with first graders. In the study reported by Neuman and Gallagher (1994), the description of the coding scheme applied to sample mother-child interactions provides a useful picture of the intervention.

Another aspect of the setting that should be attended to is the baseline conditions and those variables that might influence baseline performance. Birnbrauer, Peterson, and Solnick (1974) argue that if the investigator thoroughly explores and reports on factors that are influencing the participants' activity prior to introducing the independent variable and if the context of that activity is known, then the probability will be high that the findings from the study will generalize to other cases in which the same factors exist. This means that it is incumbent upon the researcher to report carefully and precisely the baseline conditions.

In an investigation reported by Knapczyk (1991), the researcher videotaped segments from a geography class for the purpose of using these as the context for teaching ninth graders with learning difficulties to ask and answer questions in the course of teacher presentation and classroom discussion. The instruction on question asking and answering took place in a special education resource room. Not only does the use of the videotape in this study ensure that the conditions in which the students were taught the question asking–answering strategies closely approximate those for which the researcher had designed the intervention but, furthermore, if there were a failure to generalize from the resource room to the general education setting, the videotapes would have been useful for determining similarity between baseline conditions and those in place during the generalization phase of the research.

Lincoln and Guba (1985) have argued that, ultimately, the burden of proof for generalizability rests less with the investigator than with the reader. Nevertheless, the thick description that is typically associated with qualitative research can support the readers' attempts to bridge the gap between the reported research and the application settings with which they are concerned. This also can—or should—be the case with single-subject experimental research.

Characterizing the Measures

The conceptualization and the operational definition of the measures are important considerations in generalizing experimental results. The issues related to measures used in single-subject designs are not unique to this methodology: biased measurement, unreliable measures, and measures that yield floor and ceiling effects clearly constitute threats to many methodologies. The repeated measures incorporated in single-subject designs can, however, satisfactorily address some measurement concerns. For example, the baseline phase provides a test of the reliability of the measures in place. In addition, since the investigator is examining the baseline data for the purpose of determining whether a clear picture has emerged regarding the behavior of interest, floor and ceiling effects become more evident.

To illustrate, Palincsar, Brown, and Campione (1993) experienced floor effects during baseline when they began their investigation of reciprocal teaching with first graders. As described earlier, in this series of studies, the texts were read aloud to the students, and the students were asked to respond to an array of questions that asked them to recall information, to apply the information heard to the solution of a novel problem, to identify the gist of the text, and to draw inferences from the text. One subset of students experienced considerable difficulty with this form of assessment, consistently earning scores of 0 to 10 percent. Anticipating that these floor effects would hinder characterizing these students' learning once the intervention was in place, the researchers modified the assessment by interjecting the questions throughout the reading, thereby reducing the demand on the children's memory and enabling them to reveal more about their understanding of the text.

Analytic Generalization

There is another form of generalization that is not founded on populations, settings, or measures but rather rests on generalizing a particular set of results to a theory—a process that Yin (1989) refers to as "analytic generalization." Generalizing to a theory means providing evidence that supports that theory (Firestone, 1993). When generalizing to a theory, one uses the theory to make predictions and then confirms those predictions. In this case, replications under conditions identical to those in the initial investigation serve to support the reliability of the theory; the conditions that are in place are referred to as the *scope conditions* limiting the generalizability of the theory. When the conditions vary from those that were originally in place, then the successful replication contributes to the generalizability of the theory and attests to its robustness.

In our search of the literature in literacy research that used single-subject designs, we found several cases in which the researchers explicitly identified the theory guiding the design of the intervention, enabling analytic generalization. For example, Idol and Croll (1987) developed their story-mapping intervention guided by schema theory, suggesting that the correspondence between a reader's underlying knowledge structures (schemata) and the textual information determines the extent of comprehension. Relevant schemata lead the reader to appropriate inferences, in turn facilitating comprehension and retention of the text. Guided by this theory, Idol and Croll implemented a story-mapping intervention, using a multiple-baseline across-participants design in which students were in baseline from four to ten days, during which they read and retold a story and responded to comprehension questions regarding the story. During the intervention phase, the teacher modeled using a story map to identify components of narratives (character, setting, goal, and so on). The intervention continued until the participants successfully responded to 80 percent of the comprehension questions. Following this, there was a return to the baseline condition in which the students independently read and retold stories. The results of their work provided some support for schema theory to the extent that the participants showed demonstrable and robust gains on the comprehension measures that explicitly called for drawing relationships between the structural schemata (story-map components) and the reading materials when responding to comprehension questions that were organized around the story components. However, the evidence for schema theory was weaker when the assessment procedure called for retelling the story. On this measure, students did not consistently use the story components to support their retellings. Furthermore, only a subset of the students indicated improved comprehension when reading classroom materials that were more difficult than the materials used during instruction. This study, it could be argued, provides partial support for schema theory with scope conditions including a close match between the method of instruction and the method of assessment, as well as a close match between the instructional and assessment materials.

Conclusions

Contemporary discussions of science suggest that the results of research activity are knowledge claims that compete to gain acceptance by a community (cf. Polkinghorn, 1983). Our assumptions that "truth" is the fruit of carefully following prescribed methodology have been tempered by recognition that, in fact, the most a particular proposal may represent is the best available evidence. It is the community, through a process of practical reasoning, that determines the merits of the proposal.

Single-subject methodology is clearly one tool that has the potential to contribute to meaningful understanding of subjects of inquiry. In particular, this methodology offers the opportunity to examine the responses of individuals, including the variability that occurs within as well as among individuals. In this chapter, we have suggested ways in which single-subject methodology can be used to gather evidence in a manner that is more likely to result in the community viewing that evidence as useful; namely, we have proposed considerations that enhance the internal and external validity of this methodology.

References

Birnbrauer, J.S., Peterson, C.R., & Solnick, J.V. (1974). Design and interpretation of studies of single subjects. *American Journal of Mental Deficiency, 79*(2), 191–203.

Campbell, D.T., & Stanley, J.C. (1963). *Experimental and quasi-experimental designs for research*. Chicago, IL: Rand-McNally.

Danziger, K. (1990). *Constructing the subject*. Cambridge, UK: Cambridge University Press.

Firestone, W.A. (1993). Alternative arguments for generalizing from data as applied to qualitative research. *Educational Researcher, 22*(4), 16–23.

Graham, S., & Harris, K.R. (1989). Improving learning disabled student's skills at composing essays: Self-instructional strategy training. *Exceptional Children, 56*(3), 201–214.

Hersen, M., & Barlow, D.H. (1976). *Single case experimental designs: Strategies for studying behavior change*. New York: Pergamon.

Idol, L., & Croll, V.J. (1987). Story-mapping training as a means of improving reading comprehension. *Learning Disability Quarterly, 10*, 214–229.

Knapczyk, D. (1991). Effects of modeling in promoting generalization of student question asking and question answering. *Learning Disabilities Research and Practice, 6*, 75–82.

Kratochwill, T.R. (1978). *Single subject research: Strategies for evaluating change*. New York: Academic.

Lincoln, Y.S., & Guba, E.G. (1985). *Naturalistic inquiry*. Newbury Park, CA: Sage.

Mudre, L.H., & McCormick, S. (1989). Effects of meaning-focused cues on underachieving readers' context use, self-corrections and literal comprehension. *Reading Research Quarterly, 24*, 89–113.

Neuman, S.B., & Gallagher, P. (1994). Joining together in literacy learning: Teenage mothers and children. *Reading Research Quarterly, 29*, 383–401.

Palincsar, A.S., & Brown, A.L. (1984). Reciprocal teaching of comprehension-fostering and comprehension-monitoring activities. *Cognition & Instruction, 1*, 117–175.

Palincsar, A.S., Brown, A.L., & Campione, J.C. (1993). First grade dialogues for knowledge acquisition and use. In E. Forman, N. Minick, & C.A. Stone (Eds.), *Contexts for learning: Sociocultural dynamics in children's development*. Oxford, UK: Oxford University Press.

Polkinghorn, D. (1983). *Methodology for the human sciences: Systems of inquiry*. Albany, NY: State University of New York Press.

Rosenberg, M.S., Bott, D., Majsterek, D., Chiang, B., Gartland, D., Wesson, C., Graham, S., Smith-Myles, B., Miller, M., Swanson, H.L., Bender, W., Rivera, D., & Wilson, R.

(1992). Minimum standards for the description of participants in learning disabilities research. *Learning Disability Quarterly, 15*, 65–70.

Wolery, M., & Exell, H.K. (1993). Subject descriptions and single-subject research. *Journal of Learning Disabilities, 26*, 642–647.

Yin, R.K. (1989). *Case study research: Design and methods* (2nd ed.). Newbury Park, CA: Sage.

Conventions for Displaying Data on Line Graphs

Sandra McCormick

The vertical (y) axis. Display on the vertical axis the values that quantify the dependent variable. If a score of 0 is possible in this set of data, place the 0 slightly above the horizontal line of the graph so that such scores will be easy for readers to discern. Show the whole range of values possible in the study (for example, if scores could have ranged from 0 to 8, use marks at equal intervals showing 0 to 8). When displaying percentages, always show the full range of values from 0 percent to 100 percent, even if no subject scores at either extreme. Place a label describing the dependent variable to the left of the vertical axis, as in Figure A.1.

Figure A.1

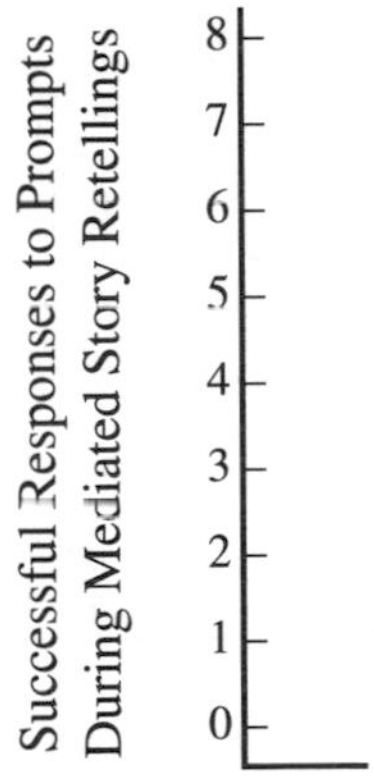

The horizontal (x) axis. This axis displays time (such as sessions or days), marked off in equal units, as in Figure A.2.

Figure A.2

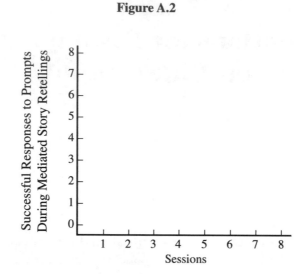

Response opportunities related to the independent variable can also be displayed on the horizontal axis. For example, a graph such as the one shown in Figure A.3 might be used if measurements were taken during 12 story retellings in a study.

Figure A.3

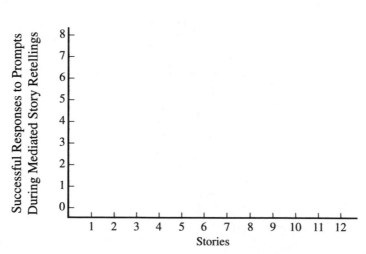

Condition (or phase) lines. Vertical condition lines show the point when a condition is changed. Labels are displayed at the top of the section for each condition. See Figure A.4 for an example.

Figure A.4

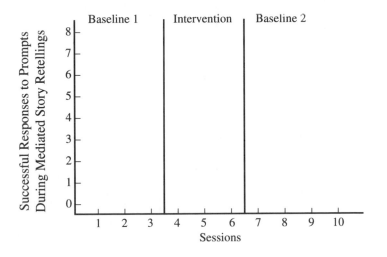

When the same condition is in effect at different times in different tiers on a multitiered graph, a broken line between the tiers indicates this circumstance. In Figure A.5, the baseline condition is in effect in tier one for trials 1 through 5, in tier two for trials 1 through 8, and in tier three for trials 1 through 10.

Data points. Data points show quantification of a response at a specific point in time. When there is one data set, data points are represented by a solid dot, as in Figure A.5. When more than one data set is displayed on a single graph, different symbols denote data points for each data set; see Figure A.6 where a solid dot, an open dot, and an open triangle are used for data points for each of three different data sets.

Data path. The data path is the connection of data points within a condition, obtained by drawing lines from one data point to the next. Data points are not connected between conditions (for example, between a baseline condition and an intervention condition); see Figure A.5 for an example. When more than one data set is displayed on a single graph, a different type of line is used for each data path; see Figure A.6, where a dashed line, a dotted line, and a combination dashed-dotted line are used for each of three different data sets.

Figure A.5

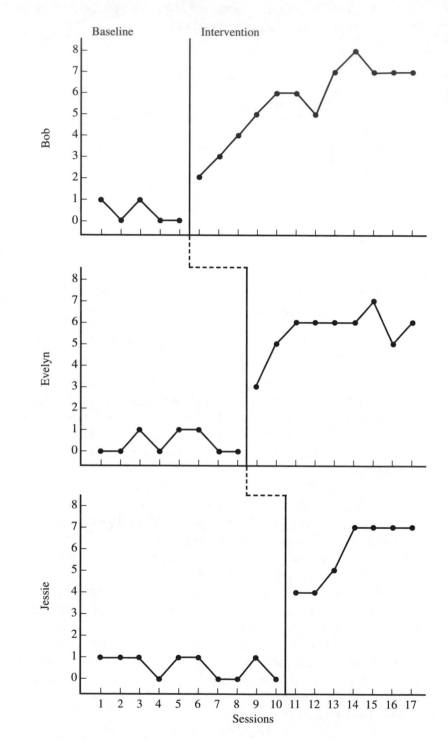

Successful Responses to Prompts During Mediated Story Retellings

Figure A.6

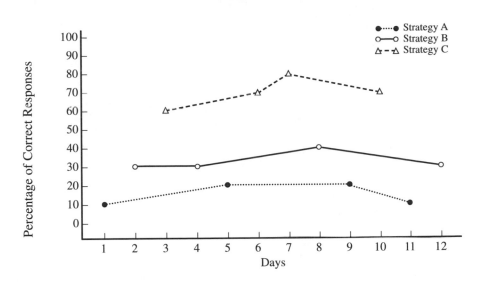

Scale breaks. Scale breaks represent a break in time when no data were collected, perhaps when a school vacation intervened or a target student was absent for a time because of illness. Data points are not connected across scale breaks. Figure A.7 provides an example.

Figure A.7

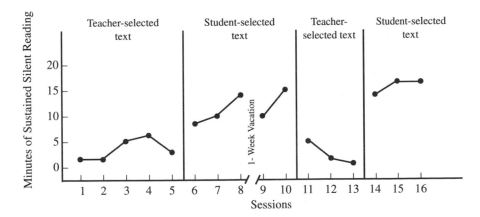

Comparison of Research Methodologies Commonly Used in Literacy Investigations

Sandra McCormick

Considering the range of questions asked in literacy research, it is recognized that variations exist within research paradigms. The purpose of this appendix is to describe typical contrasts among three global categories of investigative modes to provide a general perspective of similarities and differences. Note, however, that exceptions do occur.

Characteristic	Group-Comparison Research	Single-Subject Research	Qualitative Research
Focus on a single subject	no	yes	yes
Focus on small groups of subjects	sometimes	yes	yes
Focus on large groups of subjects	yes	seldom	sometimes
Preplanned interventions	yes	yes	sometimes
Primary focus on existing conditions	no	no	yes
Conditions carefully controlled	yes	yes	no
Use of control groups	yes	no	no
Manipulation of variables	yes	yes	no
More than one variable examined in the same study	sometimes	sometimes	yes
Personal data analysis	not usually	yes	yes
Repeated measurements to obtain baseline data before intervention begins	seldom	yes	not usually
Analysis of permanent products	yes	yes	yes
Observational recording	sometimes	yes	yes
Repeated measurement during intervention	seldom	yes	yes

Characteristic	Group-Comparison Research	Single-Subject Research	Qualitative Research
Evaluations of the intervention based on a single posttest	often	no	no
Statistical analysis of data	yes	sometimes	no
Data displayed and analyzed through graphs	sometimes	yes	no
Assessment of maintenance of learning	sometimes	yes	sometimes
Evaluation of transfer of learning	sometimes	often	sometimes
Reliability or believability of results assessed	yes	yes	yes
Conclusions drawn *during* the study	no	yes	yes
Conclusions drawn *at end* of the study	yes	yes	yes
Relatively prolonged studies	infrequently	often	often

Single-Subject Experimental Research Studies with Literacy-Related Themes

Susan B. Neuman

Studies Using Reversal Designs

Guza, D.S., & McLaughlin, T.F. (1987). A comparison of daily and weekly testing on student spelling performance. *Journal of Educational Research, 80,* 373–376.

Kosiewicz, M.M., Hallahan, D.P., Lloyd, J., & Graves, A.W. (1982). Effects of self-instruction and self-correction procedures on handwriting performance. *Learning Disability Quarterly, 5,* 71–78.

Thorpe, H.Q., & Borden, K.S. (1985). The effect of multisensory instruction upon the on-task behaviors and word reading accuracy of learning disabled children. *Journal of Learning Disabilities, 18,* 279–286.

Thorpe, H.W., Chiang, B., & Darch, C.B. (1981). Individual and group feedback systems for improving oral reading accuracy in learning disabled and regular class children. *Journal of Learning Disabilities, 14,* 332–335.

Studies Using Multiple-Baseline Designs

Multiple-Baseline-Across-Subjects Design

Bulgren, J., Schumaker, J.B., & Deshler, D.D. (1988). Effectiveness of a concept teaching routine in enhancing the performance of LD students in secondary-level mainstream classes. *Learning Disability Quarterly, 11,* 3–17. (This article is a winner of the Council for Learning Disabilities Award for Outstanding Research.)

Danoff, B., Harris, K.R., & Graham, S. (1993). Incorporating strategy instruction within the writing process in the regular classroom: Effects on the writing of students with and without learning disabilities. *Journal of Reading Behavior, 25,* 295–322.

Freeman, T., & McLaughlin, T.F. (1984). Effects of a taped-words treatment procedure on learning disabled students' sight-word oral reading. *Learning Disability Quarterly, 7,* 49–54.

Graham, S., & Harris, K.R. (1989). Improving learning disabled students' skills at composing essays: Self-instructional strategy training. *Exceptional Children, 56,* 201–214.

Graham, S., & MacArthur, C. (1988). Improving learning disabled students' skills at revising essays produced on a word processor: Self-instructional strategy training. *Journal of Special Education, 22,* 133–152.

Gurney, D., Gersten, R., Dimino, J., & Carnine, D. (1990). Story grammar: Effective literature instruction for high school students with learning disabilities. *Journal of Learning Disabilities, 6,* 335–342, 348.

Knapczyk, D. (1991). Effects of modeling in promoting generalization of student question-asking and question-answering. *Learning Disabilities Research and Practice, 6,* 75–82.

Lenz, B.K., Alley, G.R., & Schumaker, J.B. (1987). Activating the inactive learner: Advance organizers in the secondary content classroom. *Learning Disability Quarterly, 10,* 53–67. (This article, a winner of the Council for Learning Disabilities Award for Outstanding Research, provides an example of a multiple-probe design that is a variation of a *multiple-*baseline data-collection procedure.)

Lenz, B.K., & Hughes, C.A. (1990). A word identification strategy for adolescents with learning disabilities. *Journal of Learning Disabilities, 23,* 149–158, 160.

Levy, A., Wolfgang, C.H., & Koorland, M.A. (1992). Sociodramatic play as a method for enhancing the language performance of kindergarten age students. *Early Childhood Research Quarterly, 7,* 245–262.

McCormick, S., & Cooper, J.O. (1991). Can SQ3R facilitate secondary learning disabled students' literal comprehension of expository text? Three experiments. *Reading Psychology, 12,* 239–271.

Newby, R.F., Caldwell, J., & Recht, D. (1989). Improving the reading comprehension of children with dysphonetic and dyseidetic dyslexia using story grammar. *Journal of Learning Disabilities, 22,* 373–379.

Rose, T.L., & Furr, P. (1984). Negative effects of illustrations as word cues. *Journal of Learning Disabilities, 17,* 334–337.

Stevens, K.B., & Schuster, J.W. (1987). Effects of a constant time delay procedure on the written spelling performance of a learning disabled student. *Learning Disability Quarterly, 10,* 9–16.

Venn, M.L., Wolery, M., Werts, M.G., Morris, A., DeCesare, L., & Cuffs, M.S. (1993). Embedding instruction in art activities to teach preschoolers with disabilities to imitate their peers. *Early Childhood Research Quarterly, 8,* 277–294.

Multiple-Baseline-Across-Behaviors Designs

Bianco, L., & McCormick, S. (1989). Analysis of effects of a reading study skill program for high school learning-disabled students. *Journal of Educational Research, 82,* 282–288.

Mudre, L.H., & McCormick, S. (1989). Effects of meaning-focused cues on underachieving readers' context use, self-corrections, and literal comprehension. *Reading Research Quarterly, 24,* 89–113.

Neuman, S.B., & Gallagher, P. (1994). Joining together in literacy learning: Teenage mothers and children. *Reading Research Quarterly, 29,* 383–401.

Schumaker, J.B., Deshler, D.D., Alley, G.R., Warner, M.M., & Denton, P.H. (1982). Multipass: A learning strategy for improving reading comprehension. *Learning Disability Quarterly, 5,* 295–311.

Studies Using Alternating-Treatments Designs

Braithwaite, J.A. (1987). *The effectiveness of three assessment procedures to accurately predict disabled readers' word recognition.* Unpublished doctoral dissertation, Ohio State University, Columbus, OH.

Rose, T.L. (1984). The effects of two prepractice procedures on oral reading. *Journal of Learning Disabilities, 17,* 544–548.

Rose, T.L., & Beattie, J.R. (1986). Relative effects of teacher-directed and taped previewing on oral reading. *Learning Disability Quarterly, 7,* 39–44.

Rosenberg, M.S. (1986). Error-correction during oral reading: A comparison of three techniques. *Learning Disability Quarterly, 9,* 182–192.

Studies Using a Combination of Designs

Idol, L., & Croll, V.J. (1987). Story-mapping training as a means of improving reading comprehension. *Learning Disability Quarterly, 10,* 214–229. (An example of a combination of an A-B-A design with a multiple-baseline-across-subjects design.)

Palincsar, A.S., & Brown, A.L. (1984). Reciprocal teaching of comprehension-fostering and comprehension-monitoring activities. *Cognition & Instruction, 1,* 117–175.

About the Contributors

Saul Axelrod is a professor of special education at Temple University in Philadelphia, Pennsylvania. His major interest is applying behavior analysis procedures to improving the classroom deportment and academic achievement of school children. He is the author or editor of *Behavior Modification for the Classroom Teacher, The Effects of Punishment on Human Behavior*, and *Behavior Analysis and Treatment*.

Tanja L. Bisesi is a doctoral candidate in the Department of Counseling, Educational Psychology, and Special Education at Michigan State University in East Lansing. She teaches courses in literacy assessment and learning and conducts research in the areas of classroom literacy assessment and literature-based reading instruction. She formerly worked as a speech-language pathologist in the public schools and other settings.

Judith A. Braithwaite is an educator with 25 years of experience, including 13 as a classroom teacher. For the past 14 years, she has worked as a part-time lecturer at the Ohio State University in Columbus. At present she is on a leave of absence from the Columbus (Ohio) Public Schools, working as a program developer and grant writer for the Columbus Education Association.

Michael L. Kamil is a professor of educational theory and practice at the Ohio State University in Columbus. He has been an editor of *Reading Research Quarterly*, the *Journal of Reading Behavior*, and the yearbook of the National Reading Conference. His research interests include theories and models of reading and literacy research methodology.

James Kucera is the administrator of the Tualatin Good Shepherd Lutheran Home in Tualatin, Oregon, a private corporation that provides services for people with developmental disabilities. He is also a doctoral student at Temple University in Philadelphia, Pennsylvania, where he studies the functional analysis of behavior and personnel instruction.

Sandra McCormick is a professor at the Ohio State University in Columbus, where she teaches courses in remedial and clinical reading and supervises the reading clinic. Her research interests concern instruction of students with literacy problems, especially those experiencing severe difficulties. She has conducted research using traditional group methodologies, qualitative procedures, and single-subject designs.

Susan B. Neuman is an associate professor in curriculum and instruction at Temple University in Philadelphia, Pennsylvania. She is also coordinator of the reading and language graduate program. Her research interests include family literacy and emergent literacy processes, as well as the impact of technology on literacy development. She has employed many different methodologies in her research, including meta-analysis, ethnography, single-subject design, and combinations of qualitative and quantitative methodologies.

Annemarie Sullivan Palincsar is the Jean and Charles Walgreen literacy professor at the University of Michigan in Ann Arbor, where she prepares teachers and researchers to work with students who have special needs. Her research interests include enhancing the literacy learning of students identified as learning disabled and investigating the processes of peer collaboration in problem-solving activity.

Andrea DeBruin Parecki is a doctoral student in the combined program in education and psychology at the University of Michigan in Ann Arbor. Her research interests include the education of children from minority cultures, instructional conversation, and alternative assessments of literacy.

Taffy E. Raphael is a professor in the departments of teacher education and educational psychology at Michigan State University in East Lansing. She is coordinator of the master's in literacy education program and teaches courses related to the psychology and pedagogy of literacy and methods for teaching reading and writing. Her research interests focus on creating literature-rich environments for teaching students to read, write, and talk about books, and building networks for teachers to share their research and practice in literacy education.

David B. Yaden, Jr., is currently a visiting associate professor in the School of Education at the University of Southern California in Los Angeles, where he teaches graduate courses in research methodology, the diagnosis of reading disability, and the psychological and sociocultural development of literacy. His current research interests include the early acquisition of literacy through home storybook reading and the application of nonlinear dynamical systems or chaos theory to the analysis of storybook reading conversations and literacy growth.

Contributors

Author Index

Note: An "f" following a page number indicates that the reference may be found in a figure, a "t," that it may be found in a table.

Subject Index

Note: An "f" following a page number indicates that the reference may be found in a figure, a "t," that it may be found in a table.

GRAPHS, 89, 90f; line, 21–22, 153f, 153–157, 154f, 155f; multiple-baseline, 6, 7f

GRAUNT, JOHN, 109, 110t, 111

GROUP COMPARISONS: acceptable instances, 24–25, 25f; cautious generation of, 24–25; unacceptable instances, 25

GROUP-COMPARISON RESEARCH: comparison with single-subject and qualitative research, 159–160

H

HISTORY: threat to internal validity, 139–141, 140t

I

INFERENTIAL STATISTICS, 86–87; nonparametric, 87, 94–97; parametric, 87, 90–94

INITIAL BASELINE: alternating-treatments design with, 75–78, 77f; alternating-treatments design without, 71–75, 72f; with final treatment phase, 78–81, 80f

INSTRUMENTATION: threat to internal validity, 140t, 142

INTEGRITY, 115–116

INTERINDIVIDUAL REPLICATION, 23

INTERNAL VALIDITY, 15, 116; achieving, 139–143; considerations for reversal designs, 35t; substantiation of, 15–16; threats to, 139–143, 140t

INTERRUPTED TIME SERIES WITH MULTIPLE REPLICATIONS DESIGN, 33

INTERSUBJECT REPLICATION, 23

INTERSUBJECT VARIABILITY, ix

INTERVAL RECORDING, 13

INTERVENTION: characterizing, 145–146; repetition of, 21, 22f

INTRAINDIVIDUAL REPLICATION, 21

INTRASUBJECT REPLICATION, 21

INTRASUBJECT VARIABILITY, 9

J

JOURNAL OF EXPERIMENTAL PSYCHOLOGY, 138

JOURNAL WRITING: A-B-A design study, 123–124, 125f; multiple-baseline design study, 124–126, 127f

K

KNOWLEDGE: what counts as, 110t, 111–112

L

LAG, 88, 88f

LASTING PRODUCTS: measurement grounded on, 12–13

LATENCY OF CHANGE: DETERMINING, 21

LATENCY RECORDING, 14

LINE GRAPHS, 21–22; condition or phase lines, 155, 155f; conventions for displaying data on, 153–157; data path, 155, 156f, 157f; data points, 155, 156f, 157f; horizontal (x) axis, 154, 154f; scale breaks, 157, 157f; vertical (y) axis, 153, 153f

LINEAR REGRESSION ANALYSIS, 90–91

LITERACY STUDIES: sample case-study design, 107–109; sample single-subject experimental design, 105–107; single-subject experimental research, 163–165

LOGIC: experimental, 25–28; of multiple-baseline design, 47–51

M

MAINTENANCE: assessment of, 14

MAINTENANCE MEASURES: multiple-baseline-across-behaviors design with, 55–57, 56f

MANIPULATION CHECKS, 15

MANN-WHITNEY TEST, 97

MAZE-SENTENCE TESTS, 128, 130f–131f, 132t, 133

MEAN LEVEL LINES, 18, 19f

MEASUREMENT: grounded on permanent or lasting products, 12–13; repeated, 6–8; standard procedures, 12–14

MEASURES: characterizing, 147; maintenance, 55–57, 56f

META-ANALYSIS, 98–99

MILL, JOHN STUART, 110t, 111

MODIFIED CLOZE TESTS, 128

MULTI-ELEMENT DESIGN, 66

MULTIPLE REPLICATIONS: interrupted time series with, 33

MULTIPLE-BASELINE ACROSS-BEHAVIORS DESIGNS, 49f, 52–57, 54f, 56f; studies with literacy-related themes, 165

MULTIPLE-BASELINE ACROSS-SETTINGS DESIGNS, 60–61, 61f

MULTIPLE-BASELINE ACROSS-SUBJECTS DESIGNS, 57–58, 59f; studies with literacy-related themes, 163–165

MULTIPLE-BASELINE DATA: randomization test for, 97

MULTIPLE-BASELINE DATA-COLLECTION: studies with literacy-related themes, 164

MULTIPLE-BASELINE DESIGNS, 47–63; advantages and limitations, 62–63; constraints in using, 50–51; examples, 48–50, 49f, 124–126; logic of, 47–51; studies with literacy-related themes, 163–165; tip sheet for, 51t

MULTIPLE-BASELINE GRAPHS, 6, 7f

MULTIPLE-INTERVENTION INTERFERENCE: threat to internal validity, 140t, 142–143

MULTIPLE-SCHEDULE DESIGN, 66

MULTIPLE-TREATMENT INTERFERENCE, 81

N

NONPARAMETRIC ANALYSIS, 94–97; tests, 87, 97

O

OBSERVATION: threat to internal validity, 140t, 142

OBSERVATIONAL RECORDING, 13

OBSERVER'S CHECKLISTS, 16; sample, 17f

ORDINAL PATTERN ANALYSIS, 97

P

PARAMETRIC ANALYSIS, 87, 90–94

PARTICIPANTS: characterizing, 145

PERMANENT (OR LASTING) PRODUCTS: measurement grounded on, 12–13

PERSONALIZED EVALUATION OF DATA, 3–5

PHASE LINES, 155, 155f

POSITIVISM, 137

POSTPOSITIVISM, 137

PRACTICALISTS: view of combining alternative research paradigms, 110t, 112–113

PRAGMATISTS: view of combining alternative research paradigms, 110t, 112–113

PREDICTION, 27

PREVIEWING, 64–65

32; repetitions of baseline and intervention conditions in, 21, 22f; studies with literacy-related themes, 163, 165; variations, 37–44

S

SCALE BREAKS, 157, 157f

SCIENTIFIC PROCEDURE: what counts as, 110t, 111

SCOPE CONDITIONS, 147

SCORES: ascertaining reasons for differences between, 91–92; hypothetical A-B, 94–95, 95t

SERIAL DEPENDENCY, 87

SETTING: CHARACTERIZING, 145–146

SIGN TEST, 97

SIMULTANEOUS TREATMENT DESIGN, 66

SINGLE-SUBJECT DATA ANALYSIS: examples, 89–99; questions to ask about, 99–102; special problems in, 87–89

SINGLE-SUBJECT DESIGNS: characteristics of, 106t; classroom use, 120–136; combining with qualitative research, 104–119; sample studies, 105–107, 122–134; statistical analysis procedures, 84–103; teachers' use, 120–136

SINGLE-SUBJECT EXPERIMENTAL RESEARCH, 1–31; advantages of, 117; applications, 28–30; basic procedures, 2; vs case studies, ix; comparison with group-comparison research and qualitative research, 159–160; efficiency of, 29; features of, 3–28, 105–109; important issues related to, 137–150; purposes of, 1–3; rationale for, ix-x; studies with literacy-related themes, 163–165

SINGLE-SUBJECT RESEARCH (term), 4

SINGLE-SUBJECT–CASE-STUDY COMBINATION DESIGNS, 113–114, 117–118; advantages, 114–117; studies with literacy-related themes, 165

SOCIAL VALIDITY, 114

STABILITY: data, 8–12

STATISTICS: considerations for, 102; descriptive, 86–87; examples, 89–99; high-inference strategies, 100; inferential, 86–87; low-inference strategies, 100; nonparametric, 87, 94–97; parametric, 87, 90–94; procedures for single-subject designs, 84–103; questions to ask about, 99–102; results, 101–102; selection of procedures, 86–87, 100–101; special problems, 87–89; use in single-subject designs, 85–86; visual, 16–22, 89–90

SYSTEMATIC REPLICATION, 35t

T

T TESTS, 87; use of, 92–93

TEACHER-PRONOUNCED TESTS, 128, 130f–131f, 132t, 133

TEACHER-RESEARCHERS, 120–122, 134–136; benefits of, 122; rationale for, 121–122

TEACHERS: sample single-subject design studies by, 122–134; using single-subject designs in classroom, 120–136

TEST SCORES: ascertaining reasons for differences between, 91–92